LOST SKI AREAS

of the

Southern Adirondacks

JEREMY K. DAVIS

THE History PRESS

LOST SKI AREAS MAP

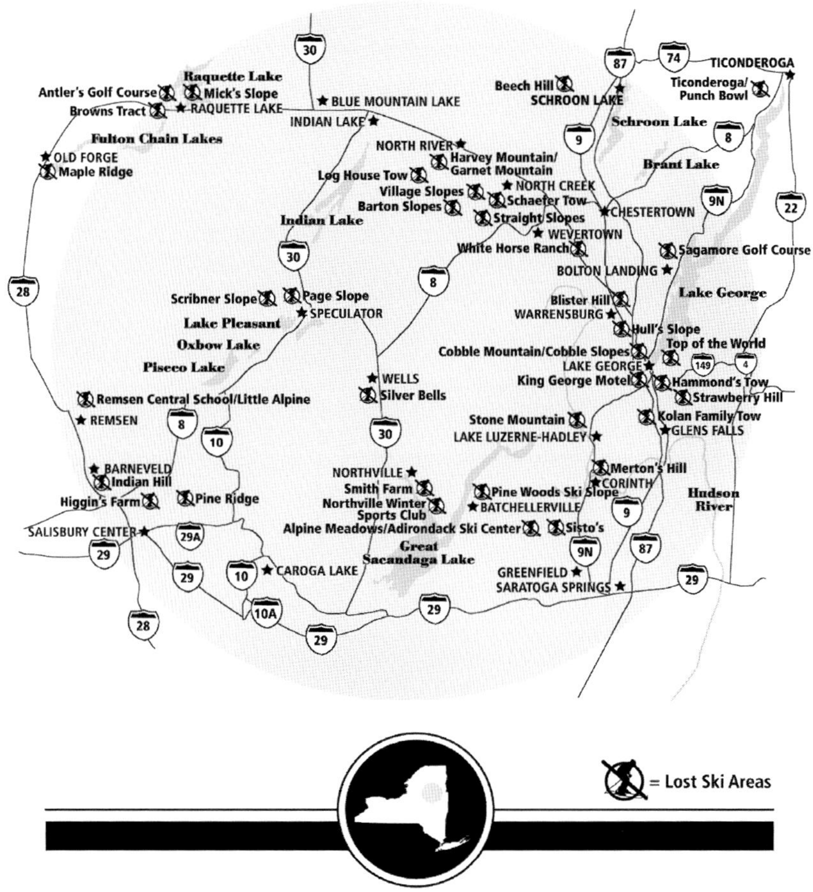

Thirty-eight ski areas that once operated in the Southern Adirondacks have now become lost. Almost every town and village had a ski area at one point, from small rope tow slopes to larger areas with nearly one thousand feet of vertical drop. While no longer in operation, these lost ski areas have contributed greatly to the sport across the region, and their influence is still being felt today by all those who enjoyed them. This map shows the approximate location of all the lost ski areas in this book. *Map designed by Scott Cahill.*

Published by The History Press
Charleston, SC 29403
www.historypress.net

Cover photos courtesy of Jon Regan, Ticonderoga Historical Society (Hancock House), Historical Society of Lake Pleasant and Speculator, Town of Webb Historical Association, Jim Ehrensbeck, Linda Jo (Taylor) Stevens, Ann Butler and Greg Schaefer.
All images are courtesy of the author unless otherwise acknowledged.

First published 2012

Manufactured in the United States

ISBN 978.1.60949.384.4

Library of Congress CIP data applied for.

Notice: The information in this book is true and complete to the best of our knowledge. It is offered without guarantee on the part of the author or The History Press. The author and The History Press disclaim all liability in connection with the use of this book.

This book is dedicated to all the founders and their families, ski instructors, ski patrol, employees and skiers of ski areas now lost. Their enterprising spirit, hard work and love of skiing have made a tremendous impact throughout the Southern Adirondacks and will not be forgotten.

CONTENTS

ACKNOWLEDGEMENTS

This book would not exist if not for all the people and organizations that helped contribute to it. From memories of those who skied the lost areas, to the families who operated them, to historical societies and individuals that allowed me to use their photos, I thank you.

The History Press is an excellent partner in the publishing business. Its design, marketing, sales and editing staff are top notch. I appreciate my commissioning editor, Whitney Tarella, for all her help with the proposal, writing and editing of this book. I have also enjoyed working with Dani McGrath, Hilary Parrish and Jamie Barreto at The History Press over the last few years.

The following people/organizations provided the images for the book: Bill Bennett, Ann Butler, Polly Butler-Jette, Elaine Carlin, Don Clemmons, Gail Cramer, Bronwyn Davis, Bea Evans, Roger Friedman, Historical Society of Lake Pleasant and Speculator, Paul Imrie, Johnsburg Historical Society, Kingsley family, Mary Joan Castle Kurimski, Mannix Publishing, New England Ski Museum, Steve Parisi, Mark Pavlus, Bruce Phelps, Jon Regan, Marjorie Near Roberts, Salisbury Historical Society, Michelle San Antonio, Greg Schaefer, Linda Jo Taylor Stevens, Ron and Arlene Strader, Ticonderoga Historical Society (Hancock House), Town of Northampton Archives, Town of Remsen, Town of Webb Historical Association, Warrensburgh Historical Society, Annie Weaver and Larry Wilke.

Scott Cahill designed the wonderful maps of lost, restored and open ski areas throughout the region. His patience and hard work creating these maps are greatly appreciated!

Acknowledgements

The history of the Gore Mountain region lost ski areas could not have been completed without the help of Larry Wilke. Larry researched many of the lost ski areas in that region for an exhibit on display at the North Creek Depot Museum and showed me all their locations. It was fun exploring all those areas, and Larry was an excellent guide. His wife, Sally, also was a great host when on my visits. The Schaefer family, long tied to the Gore Mountain region, was also invaluable. Greg and his wife, Ellen, Bill, Penny, Chris and Bud all helped me to better understand Carl Schaefer and his impact on ski area development in the area.

Several other people also took the time to show me the specific locations of former ski areas. Karen Usselmann showed me around Pine Ridge in Salisbury Center and pointed out the location of Gold Mine Hill. James Kammer gave me a tour of the Raquette Lake ski areas. Bill Dolback pointed out the location of the Punch Bowl in Ticonderoga. Bruce Phelps gave a great tour of Little Alpine in Remsen. I enjoyed exploring Harvey Mountain and the North Creek Ski Bowl with Andy Dufresne.

The following provided valuable fact checking, extensive details on lost ski areas or put me in contact with those who had more information: Bill Van Allen, Eva Anderson, Bill Bennett, Peter Billard, Ann Butler, Polly Butler-Jette, Bronwyn Davis, Bill Dolback, Jim Ehrensbeck, Bea Evans, Deborah Evans, Ron Farra, Mary Alice Hallett, Bernard Haskell, Cathy Hay, Patricia Hill, Donna Kagiliery, Mike Marnell, Peg Masters, Gail Murray, Steve Parisi, Bruce Phelps, Bill Schaefer, Bud Schaefer, Chris Schaefer, Greg Schaefer, Linda Jo Taylor Stevens, Ron and Arlene Strader, Annie Weaver and Larry Wilke.

Digital newspaper archives available at www.fultonhistory.com and www.nnyln.org were extremely helpful in discovering many facts and stories of these areas. Those sites and the ease of access to historical articles made understanding the history of lost ski areas so much easier.

Special thanks to my family, which has been very encouraging in this project. My fiancé, Scott Drake, has been very supportive and accompanied me on several explorations of lost ski areas. My parents, Ken and Linda Davis, have encouraged my passion for lost ski areas for more than twenty years. My brother and sister-in-law, Nathan and Stephanie Davis, have also been there to support the research.

INTRODUCTION

The Southern Adirondack region of New York has long been a favorite of winter sports enthusiasts. The combination of beautiful mountains, frozen lakes and deep snow cover provides the landscape for all kinds of outdoor activities. Many tourists and residents alike enjoy snowshoeing, ice skating, hockey, ice fishing, tobogganing, cross-country skiing and, of course, downhill skiing. While skiing has been popular for well over a century, the growth of organized downhill ski areas has been somewhat more recent, beginning about seventy-five years ago.

Downhill ski areas developed in the improbable era of the Great Depression. New Yorkers were looking for an escape, an affordable way to beat the winter blues. Skiing began to appeal to the masses, as once skis were purchased, the sport became essentially free. All one needed to do was find a nearby hill, climb up, strap on the skis and ride down. More thrills were needed though, as short hills could only go so far. The 1932 Olympics in Lake Placid provided a huge boost, exposing many residents to the excitement and energy of winter sports.

Ski clubs gradually formed across the state and in towns across the Adirondacks in the early to mid-1930s. These ski clubs cut trails, often working with government groups such as the Civilian Conservation Corps. The first trails were narrow, twisting and required a lot of effort to climb to the top in deep snow. At most, skiers could make a handful of runs each day before exhaustion would set in. An alternative to climbing was sought.

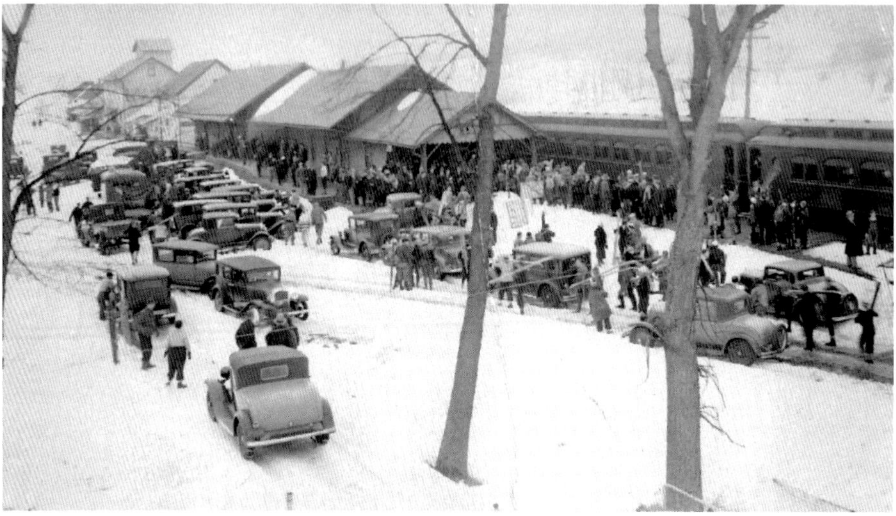

After arriving from Schenectady aboard the Adirondack's first snow train on March 4, 1934, skiers boarded buses and headed for the ski trails. Some went to the non-lift-served Village Slopes, while others rode on trucks to higher ski trails on the shoulder of Gore Mountain. With this first snow train, ski area development began in earnest across the Adirondacks, and Carl Schaefer would construct New York State's first rope tow during the fall of 1935 at the Village Slopes in North Creek. *Courtesy of Greg Schaefer.*

With a decent railroad infrastructure into the heart of the Adirondacks, the concept of a snow train was developed. One ski club, the Schenectady Wintersports Club, arranged a snow train to the village of North Creek on March 4, 1934. Hundreds of skiers traveled from Schenectady to North Creek onboard the train and flooded the village. From there, trucks would pick up passengers and drive them to the backside of Gore Mountain, where a variety of trails would take them back to the village. Several long runs could be completed in a day without the tiring climb. Skiers were thrilled, and snow trains became very popular for the next ten years.

The first actual ski lift that did not involve a moving vehicle was built at the Over the Ridge Slopes in North Creek for the 1935–36 season. Carl Schaefer constructed the first tow a short walk from North Creek, based on a lift at Woodstock, Vermont. At this fledgling ski area, truly the first lift-served in New York State, skiers could now take dozens of run in a day. Sure, their arms would be exhausted and their mittens shredded by the end of the day, but they would have had a tremendous amount of fun.

Rope tows sprouted across the Southern Adirondacks for the rest of the 1930s, as more snow trains brought skiers to destinations in Ticonderoga,

North Creek and Old Forge. A more modern ski lift, a J-bar, was even built in Lake George. The growth potential seemed unlimited as more and more towns and private enterprises built lifts, cleared slopes and trails and became destinations. Ski clubs were founded in almost every town and worked hard to promote their own individual areas. Otto Schniebs, a famous German ski instructor, founded the American Ski School out of Lake Placid and employed many instructors who taught countless to ski.

Then World War II broke out. Many ski areas closed due to rationing, as well as a shortage of employees, as many of their operators were fighting in the war. The few that did stay open limited their hours, and few snow trains ran during this period.

However, the good times would once again return across the region once the war ended. Tenth Mountain Division soldiers wanted to continue to enjoy a mountain lifestyle and began to become affiliated with ski areas. They opened up their own mountains, joined ski patrols at existing ones or took their families out to enjoy them.

Next, the new generation of baby boomers in the 1950s and 1960s began to learn the sport from their parents. More family ski areas with medium-sized facilities—such as Harvey Mountain in North Creek—opened during this period of time. These catered to a less hectic crowd and appealed to skiers who wanted to enjoy the sport in a safe environment. A new resort, the state-owned Gore Mountain, opened and expanded during the 1960s and gave skiers a much larger ski experience.

The 1970s brought about the bursting of the ski area bubble, as inflation, gas shortages, high insurance rates, competition and even vandalism all began to take their toll. Ski areas closed one by one, succumbing to these pressures. Their lifts were either sold off or were left on site to rust. Trails grew back in, and once active areas faded away. By the 1990s, a majority of the ski areas in this book had closed and began to become distant memories. Thirty-nine ski areas have now become lost, with little chance of revitalization.

This book chronicles the history of all the lost ski areas in the Southern Adirondacks. The region was defined as being south of a line from Ticonderoga to Blue Mountain Lake and to the Western Adirondacks and south to the foothills. This includes a few areas just outside the "Blue Line" but that were closely affiliated to the Adirondacks.

As long as each ski area had an uphill lift that was not a vehicle, it was counted as a lost ski area. Some rope tow areas were very small, with verticals under one hundred feet. Other areas were much larger, nearing one thousand vertical feet with a few dozen trails. A detailed account of their development, along with stories from operators, families, employees and skiers, illustrates their importance to the history of skiing in the area.

Two chapters on restored ski areas and open ski areas will discuss that all is not lost when it comes to skiing in the Adirondacks; in fact, the sport is doing quite well. Many of these open areas provide for classic skiing experiences on trails that are over fifty years old. Rates are affordable at many of these open areas, and they feature family-friendly environments.

Exploring Lost Ski Areas

Directions for each lost ski area are included in each ski area history. There are several important guidelines for exploring these areas. First, they must be on public property or be available for hiking. Please do not trespass on private property. For this book, several owners made the area available for exploration by the author for research, but these locations are not available for public viewing. Each area will specify this. Still, properties can change ownership, and it is the explorer's responsibility to make sure he is not trespassing on private property.

Second, be sure to have appropriate maps, compass and GPS when checking out these areas. As many trails have now become obscured, it is quite easy to become lost. Third, be sure to leave any and all artifacts from the ski area on site so that others may enjoy them. Finally, many of these areas are no longer suitable for downhill skiing. Tree growth, fallen trees, rocks and other obstacles can make a descent quite difficult.

The author recommends Harvey Mountain, Maple Ridge and Little Alpine as the easiest ski areas to explore with the least issues.

Chapter 1

LOST SKI AREAS OF THE GORE MOUNTAIN REGION

The Gore Mountain region is the epicenter of the development of downhill ski areas in the Southern Adirondacks. A total of seven lost ski areas are all found a short distance from Gore Mountain. While most were rope tow ski areas, one (Harvey/Garnet Mountain) had a T-bar and lodge. Most of the rope tow ski areas were constructed with the advent of the snow trains.

The Schenectady Wintersports Club was a driving force in the development of skiing across the area. The club was founded on November 30, 1932, by Vincent Schaefer, who became president. It tried to have a snow train to North Creek or Vermont for the 1932–33 season, but low snowfalls prevented this. The following summer, Schaefer, the Wintersports Club and the American Legion of North Creek began to clear trails on Gore and Pete Gay Mountains. Later, the North Creek Ski Club was formed to organize the trail and to build more of them. Yet another club, the Gore Mountain Ski Club, was also founded a short time later to build even more trails. Vehicles were organized to take skiers to near the summit of trails, where they would enjoy a long run back to North Creek.

Skiers began to enjoy these trails, and word quickly spread of the thrills they could provide. Bill Gluesing, a member of the Winterports Club, coined the phrase "Ride Up and Slide Down," an easy-to-remember slogan that emphasized the lack of climbing involved. In 1933, Lois Schaefer, Vincent's wife, set up a first aid committee to assist injured skiers, forming the first ski patrol in the country.

Gluesing enjoyed playing pranks on unsuspecting skiers. Once, he hauled Carl Schaefer's (Vincent's brother) stuffed bear on a toboggan to one of the trails and hid it behind a boulder. Carl and Gluesing would hide, and when a skier was spotted, they would push the bear out to near the trail using a system of pulleys and ropes. Many skiers panicked when they saw this and tried to escape but soon realized it was a fake.

On March 4, 1934, the first snow train arrived in North Creek, ushering in a new era as massive numbers of visitors enjoyed the trails. Organized by the Schenectady Wintersports Club, the train provided a very enjoyable experience to North Creek, which surely beat trying to drive on narrow, icy roads to the mountains. For the 1935–36 ski season, the first rope tow in New York was built by Carl Schaefer a short distance away from North Creek, and more areas would follow.

Most areas were associated with some kind of lodging, such as the Straight House, which had a rope tow behind the bed-and-breakfast. These establishments allowed skiers to enjoy a full weekend of skiing while remaining in one location.

Gradually, the smaller rope tow areas faded away. The North Creek Ski Bowl became the main attraction in North Creek in the 1940s and 1950s, but it was soon overshadowed by Gore Mountain. Harvey Mountain, a family ski area in North River, operated for about fifteen years in the 1960s and 1970s and provided a family atmosphere.

Schaefer Tow at Over the Ridge Slopes

North Creek, New York

1935–36

Carl Schaefer, a member of the Schenectady Wintersports Club, is credited with building the first ski tow in the Southern Adirondacks and, indeed, in all of New York State. It was his efforts that truly began the era of mechanical lift-served skiing throughout the region. While the first tow operated in its original location for just one year, it was later moved to Schaefer's own ski area, called Skiland, just to the south. Remnants of this tow exist to this day, over seventy-five years later.

After the great success of the first snow train to North Creek on March 4, 1934, and the development of ride-up-and-slide-down trails across Gore Mountain and the North Creek region, the stage was set for continued ski development in the region. A more convenient way to access ski terrain was sought. That same year, a rope tow opened in Woodstock, Vermont, the first tow in the United States. More tows would open in New Hampshire for the 1934–35 season. Stories of these rope tows made their way to the Schenectady Wintersports Club and to the Schaefer family. In February 1935, the Wintersports Club published an article in the *Schenectady Gazette* stating that a ski tow should be built and that North Creek would be an excellent location. This would start discussions, and in November 1935, plans were drawn up by Carl Schaefer to build and open a rope tow in North Creek.

The ski area was to be located on what was called "Over the Ridge," on property previously owned by Reverend McMahon of St. James Roman Catholic Church. The property was then purchased by Butler Cunningham and donated to North Creek to be used as a park. Permission was obtained by Schaefer to construct a tow. He traveled to Woodstock, Vermont, where he met with Bunny Bertram, who had built the first ski tow in the country, to inspect the operation. The story of this operation is best told in this letter from Carl Schaefer to the *North Creek News Enterprise* in August 1997, where he described the operation:

> *In the fall of 1935, I was planning the North Creek Ski School to be located at George Gregory's American Tavern where the Copperfield* [Inn] *is now. In early November, Bill Gluesing (who created the House of Magic and ran it for General Electric for decades) came to my home in Schenectady and gave me $100 and suggested I go up to the Creek and build a ski tow.*
>
> *I engaged the help of my friend, Eugene Morehouse, and the facilities and help of the Alexander Brothers' Garage. With the use of the motor from a six-cylinder 1929 Buick (cost, $25), 700 feet of hemp rope from Mahoney's hardware store in Schenectady, and bit of "engin" uity, we had the ski tow running by December 20th. The first tow was at the Ski Bowl, to the east of the current village tow. It was the first ski tow in New York state and the second in the northeast, according to my understanding.*
>
> *All the local kids had free access to the ski tow. I did ask them to back off a bit during busy time.*
>
> *At the end of the season, village fathers Ken Bennett and Howard Alexander told me that I was welcome to continue operation the next season.*

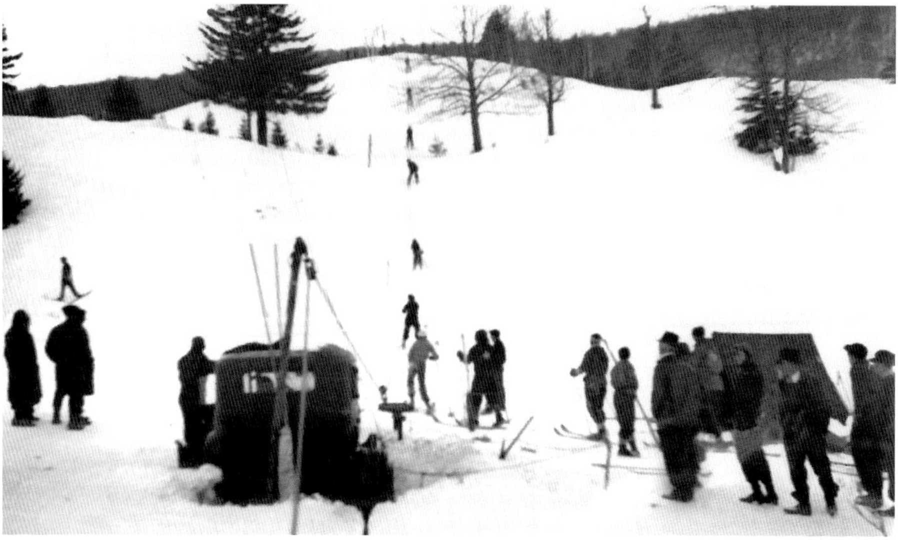

Carl Schaefer's tow, the first one installed in New York State, offered skiers a rapid ascent to several slopes punctuated by scattered trees. The ski tow was a major improvement over hiking or riding in trucks to access trails, as skiers could now make dozens of runs in a single day instead of just a handful. Spectators also came out just to see the marvel, as shown here. In 1936, Schaefer moved the tow to his property at Schaefer Skiland, where the lift operated for the public for several more years. Gore Mountain's Tubing Park is now located in the approximate location of this tow. *Courtesy of Greg Schaefer.*

> *I refrained from doing so because I was in the midst of purchasing Charlie and Edward Cross' property on the Sodom Road.*
>
> *At this point Messrs. Higgins and Burns entered the scene and had their tow operating for the 1936–1937 season, where our first tow had been.*

Tickets for the tow were quite affordable, at only twenty-five cents for ten rides. Many runs could be made in a day, and the tow was a huge success. The first snow train of the season arrived on January 1, 1936, reportedly packing the area.

As Schaefer discussed, the area changed operators, with Burt "Bucky" Burns and Emmett Higgins building their own tow on the site. The original rope tow was moved over to Schaefer's newly purchased property on the Cross Farm, which had been used as a practice slope for a few years. The story of Schaefer's Skiland, the continuation of the first tow, can be read about in this book's "Restored Ski Areas" chapter, as the Schaefer family has now rebuilt a tow on the property for their own private use.

Visiting the Area
The location of New York State's first rope tow has been greatly altered over the years and is now roughly in the same location as Gore Mountain's Tubing Park in Ski Bowl Park. The engine for the rope tow still exists on the Gore Mountain Access Road. More information on viewing this tow can be found in the chapter on restored ski areas.

Village Slopes

North Creek, New York

1936–46

After the departure of Carl Schaefer's tow, which was moved to his newly acquired property during the summer of 1936, a replacement was soon sought. In late 1936, Burt "Bucky" Burns and Emmett Higgins built a brand-new tow, sponsored by the Gore Mountain Ski Club, at the same location as the Schaefer tow. Instead of having the engine at the base of the lift, this new tow had its V-8 Ford engine at the summit. Another tow was constructed above this tow to increase the vertical and skiing terrain.

Unfortunately, the 1936–37 season was "the year with no snow," and the following one was just the same. Skiing was limited at the Village Slopes for those two seasons. The Otto Schniebs American Ski School did operate on the Village Slopes during the 1937–38 season.

In the summer and fall of 1940, the Works Progress Administration (WPA) invested $35,000 in North Creek. A ski hut was built—really a base lodge—which had been on the wish list of many local skiers since North Creek became a ski destination. It featured two levels, including a large stone fireplace that still stands today at the rebuilt base lodge in the Ski Bowl, now part of Gore Mountain. For the following season, a third rope tow erected above the previous tows to serve a slalom slope, and slopes were cleared by forest rangers. It took two months to clear the new slope, and local workmen helped clear the rest of the slopes in a week using a team of horses. The addition of the steeper slalom slope helped attract racers, and various competitions were held that year.

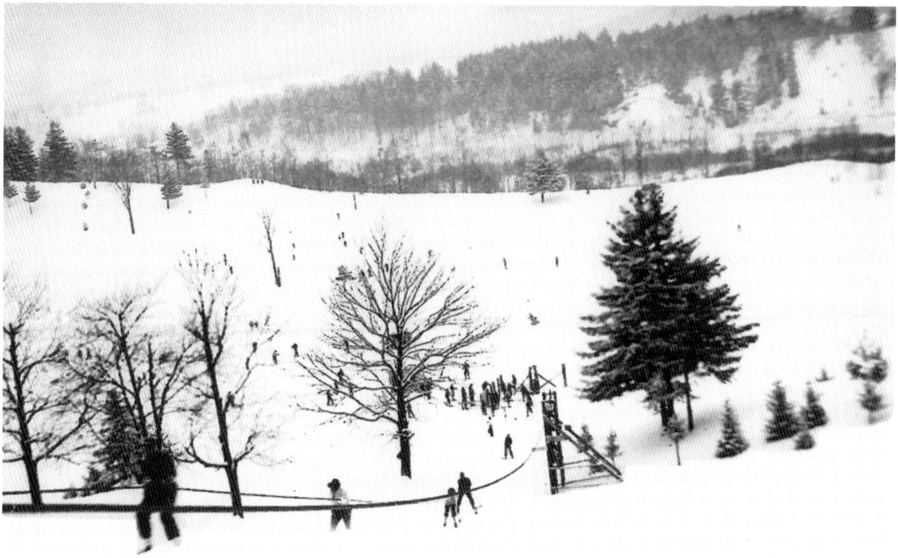

This second rope tow at the Village Slopes replaced Carl Schaefer's original rope tow in the same location. Built by Francis Burns and a Mr. Higgins in the fall of 1936, this tow's engine was located at the top of the slope. Another tow was constructed a few years later on higher slopes at the area. Today, this area is the location of Gore Mountain's Tubing Park and has been greatly altered. *Courtesy of the Johnsburg Historical Society.*

With the outbreak of World War II, usage declined at the Village Slopes, but the tows still occasionally ran. In 1946, a brand-new ski area was constructed at the site, which was now called the North Creek Ski Bowl. The tows were sold to this new development.

Visiting the Area

Today, portions of this area have been reopened by Gore Mountain as part of the Ski Bowl. Notably, the lower half of the Moxham trail was the location of the third tow at the Village Slopes. As you ski down this trail, note the newer tree growth on either side of the trail, an indication of its previous width. Other slopes are now part of the aptly named Village Slopes area, served by a triple chair. The snow-tubing park was the location of the lower tow.

Straight House Slope

North Creek, New York

1938–50

Claude Straight and his wife, Addie, operated a bed-and-breakfast on Claude Straight Road in the 1930s. The Straights were involved in raising patch beagles, dogs that were used in hunting rabbits. Their lodge, called the Straight House, was frequently visited by dog owners. Seeing the local boom in ski areas, the Straights decided to open up their own ski tow on their property in 1938. They were also good friends with Carl Schaefer, whose Skiland tow was located just across the street.

This tow was nine hundred feet in length and accessed a wide slope and two other trails. Skiers could stay slope-side at the Straight House, where they enjoyed home-cooked meals, with much of the food grown on the farm. Accommodations, which included skiing, were only three dollars a day or

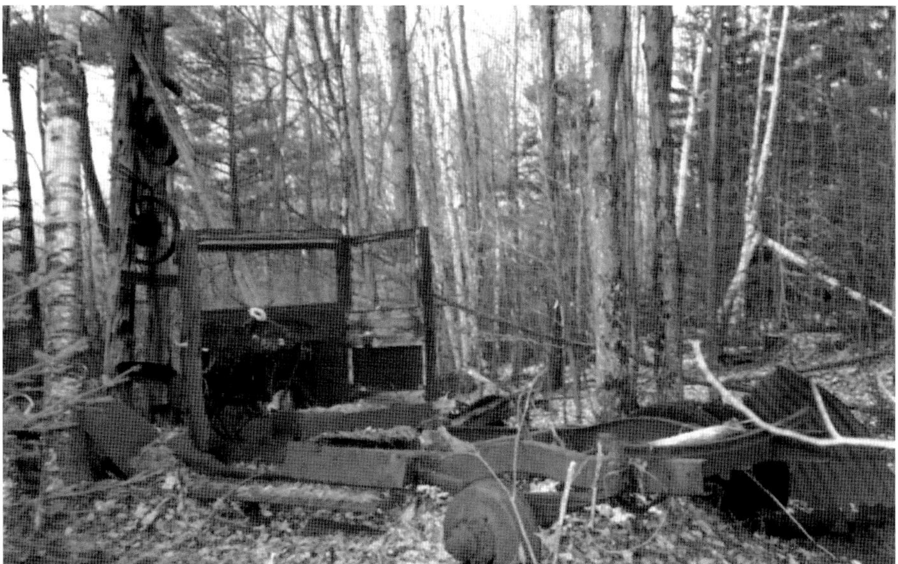

The best-preserved rope tow remnant in the Adirondacks is at Straight House Slope in North Creek. The engine, tires and pulley assembly are relatively intact in this 2004 view. Recent construction of homes has resulted in portions of the lost ski area being excavated. It is unknown how much longer the remnants of the tow will last. *Courtesy of Larry Wilke.*

twenty-one dollars a week. While other tows operated mainly on weekends, this tow operated on weekdays as well.

The Straights continued to operate the tow throughout World War II, though certainly on a limited basis. The area regained some popularity in the mid- to late 1940s, and in 1948, the Gore Mountain Ski Corporation took over the operation of the tow, as Mr. Straight was no longer able to run it. One report from 1949 shows that many farm animals were found at the bottom of the tow, including hogs, beagles, foxes, cows and sheep, which delighted skiers.

With many of the North Creek–area tows shutting down by the late 1940s, the Straight House Slope became one of the last to operate, closing around 1950. The slope gradually became overgrown, and then portions were developed into the Townridge Townhomes.

In 2011, the Chevy truck that once powered the tow remains on site, in the woods above the future condo development. Much of the truck remains, along with pulleys from the rope tow, making this one of the best-preserved rope tow engines in the Southern Adirondacks. About half of the former slope has been cleared for development, and time will tell if this remnant of ski area history will remain in place.

Visiting the Area

Now a private home development, the former rope tow is located on private property and is not accessible to the public.

Barton Slopes at Barton Mines

North River, New York

1938–51

The Barton Slopes were the starting point for many skiers on the descent to North Creek, as they were the starting point for the ride-up-and-slide-down trails. Trucks would take skiers from the North Creek Depot to the Garnet Lodge, a ten-mile trip on twisting, scenic roads. After disembarking, skiers would hike up a knoll and ski down the Half Way Brook Trail or ski down to Ives Dam and take the Roaring Brook or Rabbit Pond Trails. In addition, hearty skiers could climb to the summit of Gore Mountain and descend on the Garnet or Cloud Trails. The high elevation of these trails ensured skiing well into spring, or at least allowed skiing when lower-elevation areas had little or no snow.

Barton Garnet Mines, owned by Mr. C.R. Barton, also operated the Garnet Lodge. This location was the start for many of these ski trails. Lodging and meals were available at the lodge, and many skiers took full advantage of these facilities.

As the initial climb to access these trails would often tire out skiers before they began their descent to North Creek, another option was sought. In 1938, a 1,000-foot-long rope tow was constructed to minimize climbing. In addition, a large practice slope was cleared to the skiers' right, as well as a trail on the skiers' left. The tow was powered by a large Larrabe truck, which was located at the top of the area. With a summit elevation of 2,820 feet, the summit elevation of the Barton Slopes at Garnet Lodge was easily the highest ski lift in New York State prior to World War II.

A branch of Otto Schniebs's American Ski School opened at Barton's in the late 1930s. Schniebs himself taught lessons here and was a frequent visitor. In addition, instructor Dick Parker from the ski school also worked at the ski area.

For the 1940–41 season, a new base lodge, called the Whoopee House, was built at the bottom of the tow. Featuring a large garnet fireplace, light lunches and coffee were available here to skiers. A boardinghouse was also located nearby, used by mine workers, who also enjoyed the tow. Unfortunately, this house burned to the ground in 1944.

The Barton Cup Race—a race to North Creek—began in March 1940 at the top of the mountain, starting on the new Garnet Trail. From there, it crossed to the Cloud Trail and finished at Ives Dam. Awards were made at the Whoopee House, and the winner was Bud Hunt from Scotia in 3:37:03. He received the large silver trophy, and runners-up received cut garnets, all furnished by C.R. Barton.

World War II resulted in reduced usage of the area, but the tow became active again in the mid-1940s until about 1950. The Barton Cup was a popular event during this time. The 1950–51 season appears to have been the last at Barton's, as increased mining activity was impinging on the slope. The Whoopee House was placed on skids and moved down to the entrance gate on Barton Mines Road, where it continues to operate today as a mineral shop and a jumping-off point where tourists can visit the mines and dig for their own garnet.

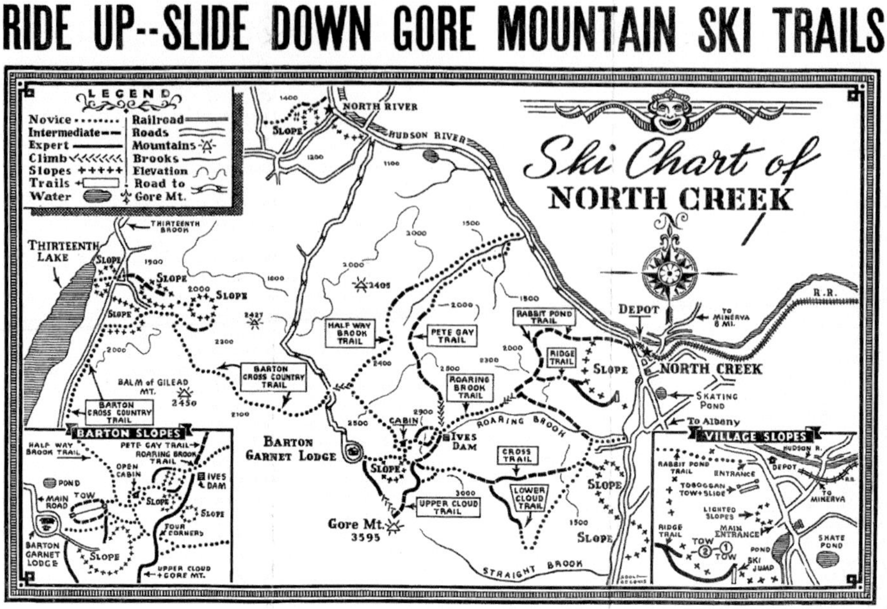

The North Creek region featured many ski trails and tows during the 1930s. This map shows the various non-lift-served trails, such as Rabbit Pond, Roaring Brook and Pete Gay, along with tow operations at the Village Slopes and Barton Slopes. Note the two tows depicted in the Village Slopes. The Barton Slopes tow served a wide-open slope and also provided access to other trails. *Courtesy of Larry Wilke.*

Throughout the 1950s, the rest of the ski trails from the property down toward North Creek decreased in popularity. Towers for the rope tow were removed, but the Larrabe truck remained. Trees encroached on the open slope and rendered it nearly unrecognizable by the 1990s.

In May 2011, ski historian Larry Wilke and the author enjoyed an exploration of this former area. Special permission was obtained from Barton Mines to access the property, which is not open to the public. Wilke was able to find the rope tow engine, now deep in the Adirondack forest, after some searching. Unless it is someday removed, remnants of this truck could remain for another century, a testament to the early ski history of the region.

Visiting the Area

The Barton Slope is on private property and is not accessible to the public. However, one can get near the area, as Barton Mines does have tours of the mine that include the ability to treasure hunt for garnet. For more information, visit www.garnetminetours.com. In addition, skiers who ride the High Peaks Chair at Gore Mountain are only half a mile from this location and can look out across the valley to the right while riding the chairlift and see the approximate area of this former ski area.

Log House

North River, New York

1938–41

The Log House, which is now Garnet Hill Lodge, was built in 1936. It was constructed by the owner of the Hooper Garnet Mine for his son-in-law, Charles Tibbits, to be operated as a hotel. Located at a high elevation and overlooking Thirteenth Lake, the property was spectacular. With the boom in other local ski areas, a rope tow was soon built on a wide slope next to the Log House in late 1938.

At one thousand feet in length, the tow was one of the longest in the region and was powered by a six-cylinder Buick engine. A wide slope and several trails were available. For the adventurous skier, a steep descent down mine tailings provided the ultimate thrill.

Francois Bertrand, of Otto Schniebs's American Ski School, was the ski instructor for the area. A flash skier from France, Bertrand was known for driving around in a convertible with his ski outfit and white hat, according to Milda Burns, a lifelong skier who grew up in North River. Bertrand was an important asset to the ski area and was well respected. However, on a weekend in late February 1939, Bertrand was not paying attention on the rope tow and took quite a spill. He became the subject of good-natured ribbing from the rest of the guests during the weekend, as ski instructors were never seen falling over in the snow.

Guests would often stay at the Log House for a weekend or longer, with transportation provided by the lodge back and forth to the North Creek Depot. All-inclusive packages of skiing and lodging were available for five dollars a day. Square dances were a popular nighttime activity.

Milda Burns remembers that all the schoolchildren from the North River School District were provided skis, boots and poles by the school board. With

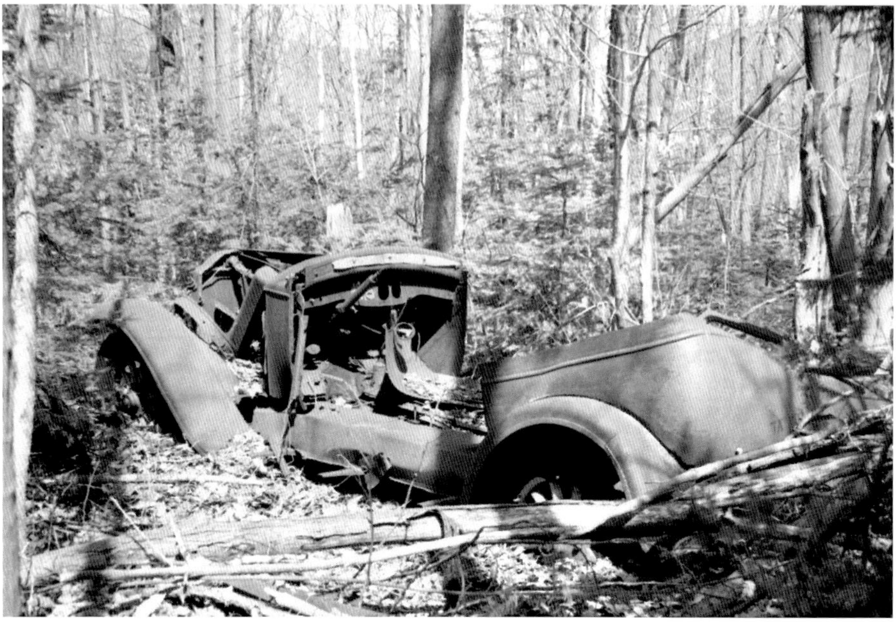

The engine for the rope tow at the Log House is all that remains after seventy years of being lost. What used to be a wide-open slope below the tow has now returned to forest. No other traces of the past ski operation remain. *Courtesy of Larry Wilke.*

skiing becoming a popular local attraction across the region, this allowed many of them to become skiers for life. She remembers that every Friday afternoon, the entire school population was driven to the Log House to ski and be taught by Bertrand.

The Log House ceased operating the ski tow during World War II and never reopened. The Log House was later renamed Garnet Hill Lodge, and cross-country skiing became its primary wintertime attraction.

Visiting the Area

Although much of the former ski slope has become reforested, the Buick that powered the rope tow remains on site. It can be clearly seen next to a playground directly in front of Garnet Hill Lodge. The lodge remains a four-season destination resort, complete with many outdoor activities such as cross-country skiing and a well-known restaurant. For more information, visit www.garnet-hill.com.

Harvey Mountain/Garnet Mountain

North River, New York

1962–77

Harvey Mountain, later known as Garnet Mountain, located on Barton Mines Road in North River, was a classic family-owned and operated ski area that lasted fifteen years, from 1962 to 1977. While modest in size (four hundred feet of vertical and a single T-bar), the ski area taught many to ski and allowed skiers to enjoy an uncrowded ski experience. Located just 2.25 miles as the crow flies from the top of Gore and just a few miles away from the North Creek Ski Bowl, competition was strong, but this area did fill a niche. Being a private ski area in the Adirondack Park, overbearing regulation regarding the area eventually resulted in Garnet Mountain closing. The land was sold to the state with the stipulation that the state would not run it as a ski area and that it would return to forever wild status.

Founder and owner Bill Butler was a salesman for the McCormick Spice Company, selling vanilla and pepper, and was based in New York City. He often traveled to New England and the Northeast. While on several business trips, he picked up the sport of skiing. Later, he had a very successful career as a management consultant and executive recruiter in New York, with clients all over the country and in Europe. His company was called E.A. Butler Associates, Inc.

On a fishing trip in the Adirondacks in early 1962, he was out exploring and went up Barton Mines Road. He came across some property that was for sale, which included a big stone house across the street from the future Harvey Mountain. This gave him the idea of owning a ski area. The land for sale was previously owned by the Barton family (which owns garnet mines up the road from the ski area), so Butler called one of the uncles of the Bartons (likely Alfred), who lived in Florida, to make an offer. Bill offered $17,000 to buy the property, paid cash on it and the land was sold quickly.

Shortly afterward, Bill and his wife, Ann, had a daughter, Polly, who was born in April 1962 while the couple was living in New York City. Ann remained mostly at home (along with their son, Robert Michael, who was three when the land was purchased) while her husband began the process of building the ski area. Otto Schniebs was brought in

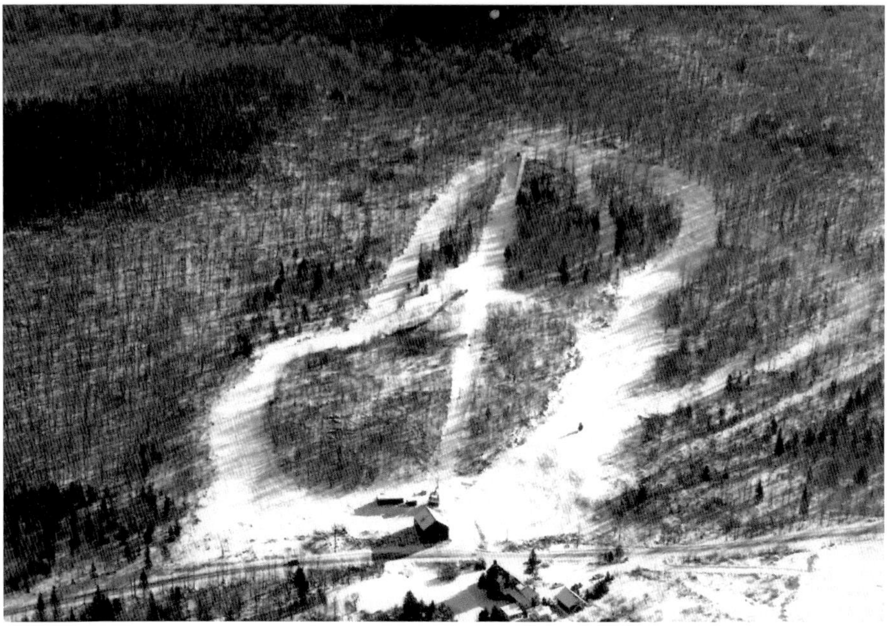

An aerial view of Harvey/Garnet Mountain reveals the compact nature of the ski area, with several choices from the summit. Most of the terrain was intermediate or beginner and catered to families. The T-bar operated right up the middle of the ski area, and you can see the wooden bridge the T-bar climbed over near the top of the ski area. Also note the wide slope to the right of the T-bar, with a single spruce tree in the middle. This tree was often used a meeting place where children would gather and then race to the bottom. *Courtesy of Ann Butler.*

to help design the ski trails. Butler then cut the trails quickly in the summer of 1962. A brand-new 1,500-foot-long Hall T-bar lift was installed that summer.

Near the base of the T-bar was a horse stable that the mine had used to house its horses. Butler converted it into a warming hut for coffee, etc. Over the next few years, it would be expanded to include light lunches. The ski area, then called Harvey Mountain, opened in December, but crowds were light the first year. In time, Butler advertised in the Glens Falls paper, radio and other outlets. Lloyd Lambert, a ski reporter based in Albany, got in touch with Butler and assisted with the promotion of Harvey in reports. Later, Lambert would hold some ski races among the kids and adults and pass out his own trophies.

The state-operated Gore Mountain Ski Center opened for the 1963–64 season, just a year after Harvey Mountain began. Competition with Gore,

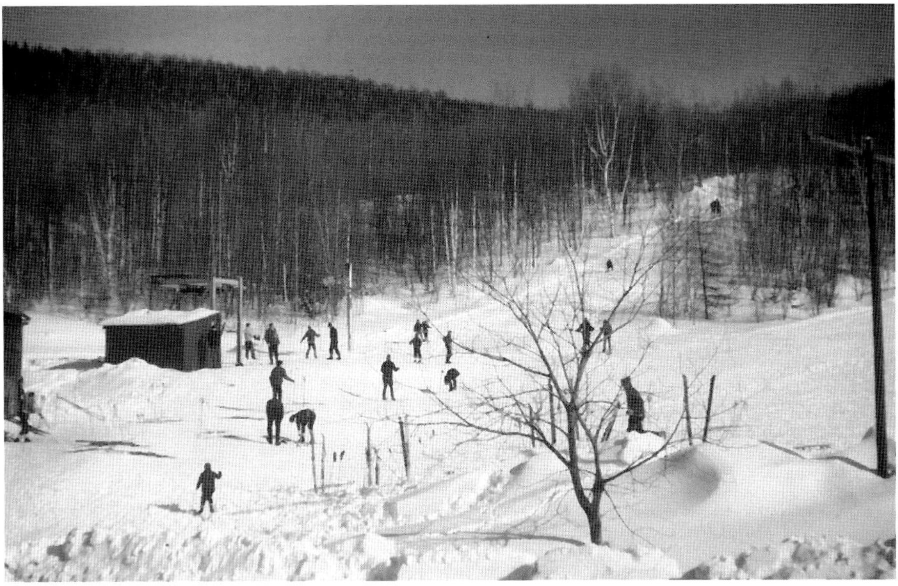

The base of Harvey Mountain was located immediately on Barton Mines Road. The bottom of the Hall T-bar is seen here, as well as the edge of the base lodge, a converted barn, on the left. The lift line remains visible today with foundations of the lift easily found, but the rest of the base area has become quite grown in. *Courtesy of Polly Butler-Jette.*

along with disputes with the state regarding signage, would ultimately result in the end of skiing at Harvey Mountain.

During its operation, Harvey and Garnet only were open on weekends, holidays and vacations, as the Butlers lived in New York City. They opened the big stone house across the street as a ski lodge where skiers could rent bunks. It had a capacity of twenty-five people, with breakfast and lunch served daily. The ski school was taught by instructor Claude Kiehn. Since Harvey/Garnet was a family-friendly place, children could learn to ski in an enjoyable environment.

Polly Butler-Jette grew up and learned to ski at Harvey and Garnet Mountain. She fondly remembers her childhood at the ski area:

> *My weekday world was a private girls' school and an apartment in New York City, so in contrast "The Lodge," as we called it, felt like total freedom. Every weekend and holiday we would get packed in the car and drive four hours north to a whole different world. A lot of my favorite memories are of my extended family and friends coming for weekends and holidays skiing*

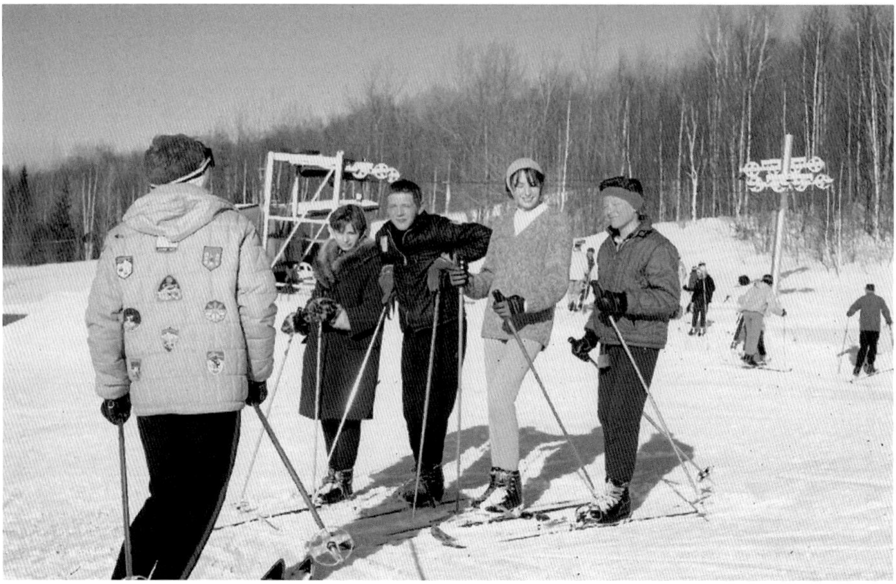

Ski lessons at Harvey Mountain began at the bottom of the T-bar. Wide-open and uncrowded slopes provided an ideal location for skiers to improve their skills. This ski instructor's jacket boasted patches from ski areas around the Northeast. *Courtesy of Polly Butler-Jette.*

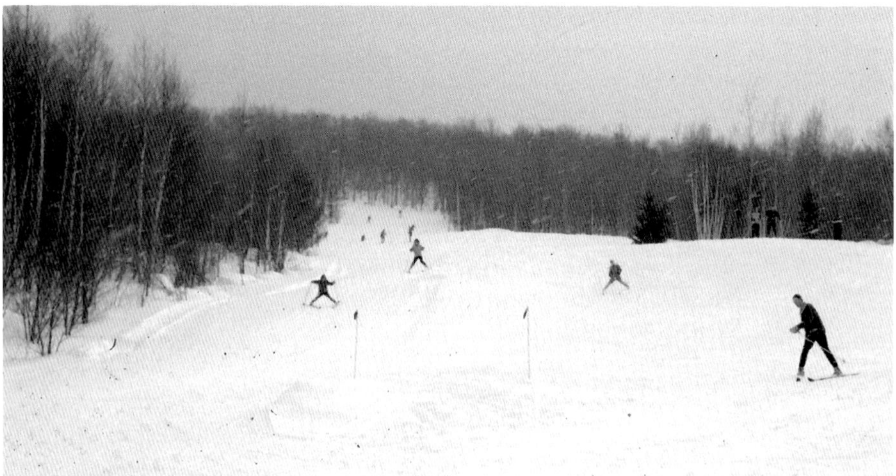

Here, skiers descend down the wide-open slope located to the right of the T-bar on a snowy day. The spruce tree mentioned in the earlier photo can be seen here on the slope. This slope has been completely reforested, but the spruce tree can still be found towering over the other trees. *Courtesy of Polly Butler-Jette.*

and then having big meals around the many picnic tables. My mom loved to do fondue parties, one of my favorites. There was always a fire in the huge garnet stone fireplace or the Franklin stove, which were the backdrops for endless games, stories and general mayhem. We would sled and play on the lower hill after the lifts closed…for hours. It was almost more fun after the lift closed.

My dad would set up ski races every week, and loyal groups of families and patrons would race each other. They gave out little bells as a weekly prize. Points would be added up at the end of the season and trophies given out. It was great fun for everyone.

On the holidays, they would always do some festive decorating on the hill. A huge red heart painted on the hill for Valentine's Day, or a huge cloverleaf for St Patty's Day. But by far my favorite was when my dad put Christmas lights on the lone small pine that sat in the middle of the main trail above the lodge. It was a center point of the ski area. It was a beautiful sight in the pitch dark of that Adirondack mountain. Music was piped in all over the mountain, either classical or German music. The song "Roll out the Barrel" will forever remind me of fun days on the slopes of Garnet. My mother and father did everything—the food, the lifts, the trails, the lodge upkeep, all of it. Of course, the hired locals helped but were hands-on for everything.

Robert Michael Butler, Polly's brother, also spent his childhood at the ski area:

With my family—mom, dad and sister—I remember trips in the car on Fridays right after school up to the North Country, often stopping in Warrensburg for groceries and of course at Oscars for bacon (lots of bacon), hamburgers to be served in the warming hut. Always the next morning we all would awake to, yes, you got it, that great smell of bacon cooking and flapjacks. We'd eat and out the door we'd go, my mom still cooking for the other guests. I would blast out the door of the lodge and go looking for my dad, who had already been out long before getting the water on in the barn warming hut and getting the T-bar checked out. He'd get that big industrial six-cylinder engine going and slowly bring that big beast of a T-bar to life. Often, I would be one of the first up the line to help set the track for the skiers who would already be arriving and making their way to the barn. Claude Kiehn, head of ski school, would be busy setting up and generally getting all of us excited about the ski day. This is where it all started for me—skiing, skiing and more skiing. From a little boy's point of view, didn't everybody grow up with a ski area in the family? I did!

As running both a ski area and a lodge became more work, the Butlers hired a housekeeper, Mary, who had previously worked at the Chatiemac Club. She did the cooking, buying supplies and laundry (which originally had to be brought back down to New York City each Sunday!). The lodge was still run until the late 1960s, when it was sold to a couple from New York City. They owned it for a year, and then the owner went to Chicago. A man from Long Island then bought the stone house but didn't maintain it properly. The first winter, he left the water on, which froze and burst the pipes. By the next winter, the house had burned down mysteriously, and that was the end of it. However, the garage is still there and is used as a hunting camp.

In the mid-1960s, Butler tried to get a sign constructed near a large sign for Gore Mountain in North Creek. Initially, the state agreed that he could put up a sign by the Conservation Department, but then it was never officially permitted. The sign was important to inform skiers nearing Gore that they could continue on Route 28 for a few miles to access Harvey Mountain. Butler had just about reached his breaking point. In March 1969, he planned to close Harvey Mountain for good, as regulations regarding signage, along with lower prices at Gore as compared to other major areas, were taking a serious toll on his business. In the end, he decided to continue ski operations. That summer, Harvey Mountain was renamed Garnet Mountain Ski Area. This was done to bring more attention to the ski area's location closer to the Barton Garnet Mines, bringing light to its location. In order to compete somewhat, they paid someone to park a truck each day near Gore Mountain with a sign advertising Garnet Mountain.

Outside of these challenges were other issues, including a few with few residents in North Creek. Some thought it was too much competition from Gore, which Ann described as "ridiculous." There was also some friction from Ski Bowl enthusiasts. Based on the large size of Gore, it is hard to believe that Harvey/Garnet was considered to be a major competitor; rather, it seems it would have been a modest alternative to a much larger resort.

The Adirondack Park Agency later made a ruling and zoned the ski area with enough restrictions that the Butlers couldn't do anything additional with their property—no homes, no more expansion, no modifications. They wished to install snow making by using water from the Balm of Gilead Stream, but the state wouldn't allow them to do so. Bill Butler did not give

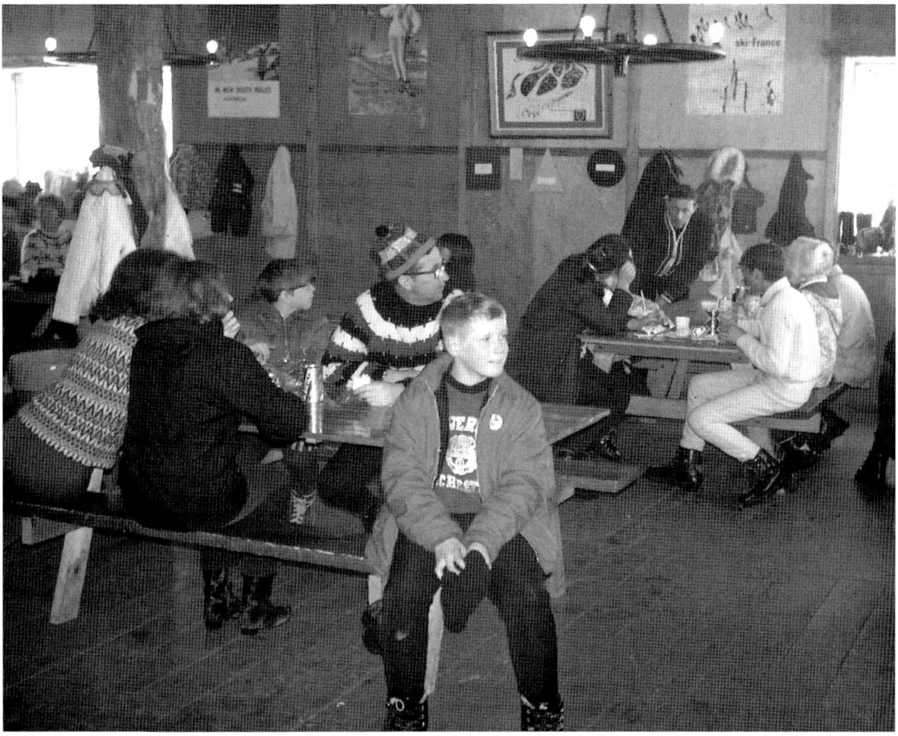

The interior of the base lodge at Harvey Mountain was a cozy spot where families could warm up between runs. It featured a small cafeteria and a large stone fireplace. Note the ski posters on the wall, including one of Harvey Mountain. Ski instructor Claude Kiehn is seen leaning over the table on the right, along with his daughter Claudia, sitting at the table in front of him. Nothing remains of the lodge today except for a concrete foundation. *Courtesy of Polly Butler-Jette.*

up fighting the state to expand or have more signs, but eventually, he realized that the state would never budge. Other ski areas were installing snow-making systems in the 1970s, but Garnet could not. Insurance rates were also on the rise. Finally, at the end of the 1976–77 ski season, Bill met with the state and sold it the land, with several stipulations:

1. The state could not run a ski area there
2. The land had to return to forever wild

The state agreed, and the area was sold and is now forever wild land. The state dismantled the T-bar lift and tore down the stable and the warming hut. The slopes were allowed to return back to forest.

The Butler children continued their family's skiing legacy by working in the industry themselves. Polly Butler-Jette works as a ski instructor at Deer Valley in Utah, while Robert Michael worked first at Deer Valley as a lift mechanic and sales representative and later in lodging management in Park City, Utah.

Visiting the Area

Harvey Mountain, while mostly reforested, remains an area that can be explored, as it is state forest preserve land. From the town of North River on Route 28, take the Barton Mines Road for 2.8 miles. The lost ski area will be on the left. Park on the road, not at the former inn location on the right, as that is private property and cannot be visited.

As you face the mountain, the still somewhat clear T-bar lift line remains visible. Other trails are hardly recognizable and take some imagination to make out. Near the base of the T-bar are foundations for the old ski lodge and T-bar control building.

The best way to explore the area is to hike straight up the T-bar line. It is a 1,500-foot-long hike to the summit of Harvey Mountain and is relatively easy, as the line is clear. You will see foundations for the lift towers on the way up. Also near the summit are wooden remnants of the elevated bridge that skiers rode over to exit the lift. Tipped over at the unload of the lift is the T-bar operator's hut.

Unfortunately, the old ski trails are quite overgrown, without much to see. It is easy to get lost on these trails, as there is little contrast between them and the surrounding woods. It is recommended that you return to your car the same way you came up the mountain via the T-bar lift line.

White Horse Ranch and Lodge

Wevertown, New York

Circa 1952–75

White Horse Ranch and Lodge, located in Wevertown, operated as a dude ranch in the 1930s. Guests would come up and ride the horses and enjoy the scenery. The ranch was located directly on Route 28 and was easily accessible. It is likely that some skiers who were enjoying the various North Creek ski areas stayed here in the 1930s and 1940s.

Around 1952, owner Jerry Stahl decided that it was his turn to cash in on the rising interest of ski areas. He built two rope tows, one a baby

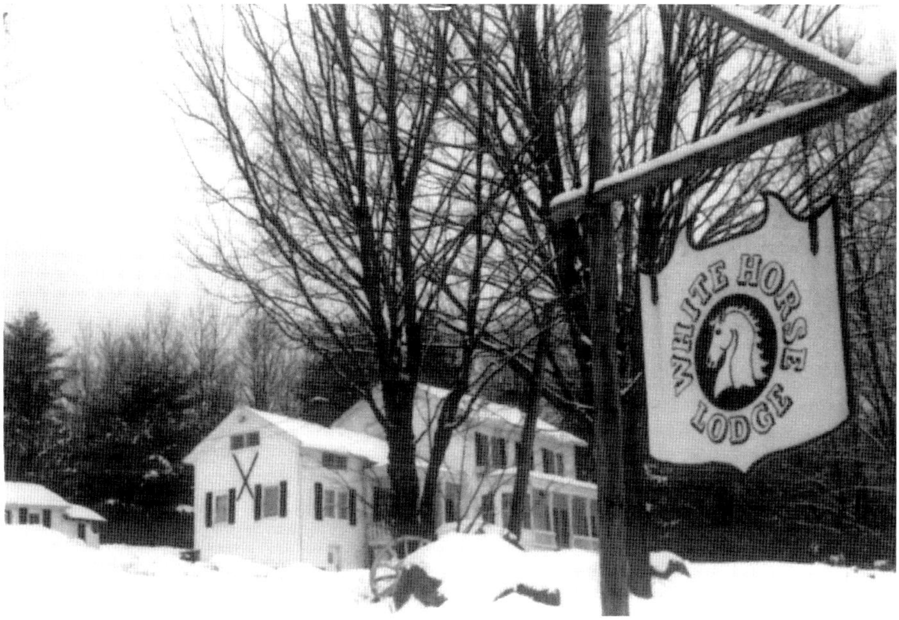

White Horse Ranch and Lodge, located directly on Route 28, focused on horses in the summer and skiing in the winter. Guests could enjoy a rope tow that served a wide-open slope behind the lodge. Note the skis mounted on the side of the lodge. While skiing is no longer offered, the lodge is now the On the Way Bed and Breakfast, where guests can still enjoy nearby Gore Mountain. *Courtesy of the Johnsburg Historical Society.*

tow powered by a Mack truck and the other a longer, more expert lift. A 1,400-foot-long slope, as well as a ski trail of the same length, was cleared. For the 1952–53 ski season, ticket prices were a dollar and a half per day or forty cents an hour. Most of the skiers were guests of the lodge, which also featured refreshments during the day.

White Horse Ranch continued to offer skiing until about 1957, when the tows were abandoned. The Mack truck engine for the lower tow was removed in the 1990s by then owner Doug Cole when he built a ski chalet on the lower slopes. The other tow engine remains to this day, high above the ranch and now deep in the forest. One rope tow pulley was mounted on a tree, and while the tree has since fallen, the pulley can still be found on the ground. The upper slope has now become reforested, though a work road can be followed to the top of the tow.

Now a bed-and-breakfast called On the Way, the former White Horse Ranch and Lodge maintains its classic charm from the past. Owned by Mark and Amy Baugh, On the Way has ski and stay packages for nearby

Gore Mountain, and guests can enjoy a hike to the former rope tow engine behind the lodge. A ski chalet is also available for rent, located on the former beginner slope.

Visiting the Area

For more information about staying at On the Way and directions, visit their website at www.onthewaybandb.com. If you are staying at the bed-and-breakfast, the owners will be happy to point out the location for the former tow.

Chapter 2

LOST SKI AREAS OF THE LAKE GEORGE–SCHROON LAKE REGION

The Lake George–Schroon Lake region contains the largest number of lost ski areas in the Southern Adirondacks. An amazing fourteen lost ski areas exist, mostly clustered a short distance away from Lake George Village. Many of these areas benefited from good access to downstate visitors. Good state roads, such as Route 9 and later Interstate 87, allowed for greater numbers of skiers to enjoy the slopes. The region is also known for having the first overhead cable ski lift in New York, a J-bar, on Cobble Mountain in Lake George. This lift was a significant improvement over the rope tows but only had a short existence before it was moved to Bromley Mountain in Vermont.

A great number of hotels had their own ski areas on site. The Top of the World Resort in Lake George offered a short rope tow but a beautiful view of the lake. The Sagamore Hotel, an improbable location for a ski tow, once had a beginner's rope. Town-operated ski areas, such as Stone Mountain in Lake Luzerne and Blister Hill in Warrensburg, provided very affordable locations for residents to learn and enjoy the sport. These two areas succumbed to heavy vandalism, which was constant in the 1970s.

The snow trains were not as active in this region as they were in Old Forge or North Creek, with Ticonderoga being an exception. There, despite a tremendous effort to build a ski complex, a lack of natural snowfall and southeast-facing slopes doomed the project, and the area is not known for skiing today.

COBBLE MOUNTAIN

Lake George, New York

1937–41

It is hard to believe today that Lake George was once the location of a pioneer ski area with a lift that was unmatched in the state of New York. This ski area was located on Rattlesnake Cobble, a ridge on Prospect Mountain. In 1936, the Winter Sports Club of Lake George purchased a large tract of land on the Cobble with assistance from local and Glens Falls businesses. Ski trails had previously been cut on the mountain in the early-mid 1930s, but it was not until the winter of 1937–38 that a ski lift was installed.

The lift—what is now referred to as a J-bar but was then called just an "overhead cable tramway"—was installed by Fred Pabst Jr., the owner of Ski Tow Incorporated. In the late 1930s, Mr. Pabst owned or operated ski areas in such diverse locations as Iron Mountain, Michigan; Wausau, Wisconsin; and Plymouth, New Hampshire. He was the first person to own a chain of ski areas and was well ahead of his time.

Constructed during the summer of 1937, the J-bar off Cooper Street on Cobble Mountain was 2,400 feet long and served a vertical drop of 500 feet. A huge "ski-tow" sign directed skiers to the slope from the village of Lake George. A wide-open slope 500 feet wide and with a maximum pitch of thirty-four degrees provided a good challenge for skiers. The slope was located quite close to the bottom of the former incline railroad that had served the summit of Prospect during the earlier portions of the century. Additional trails were constructed with such names as Sky Way, Will Wood and the Indian Trail, though some of those required a hike to the summit first.

The ski lift was so novel that numerous articles had to describe how to use it, as skiers at that time were used to either rope tows or simply hiking to the summit. An article in the 1939 *Schenectady Gazette* described how to ride the lift:

> *This pusher-type tow as you doubtless know is the one with the overhead traveling steel cable from which dangle a large number of wooden arms with a horizontal cross piece at the bottom. To get on, the system is to place yourself in front of an oncoming arm in plenty of time. You*

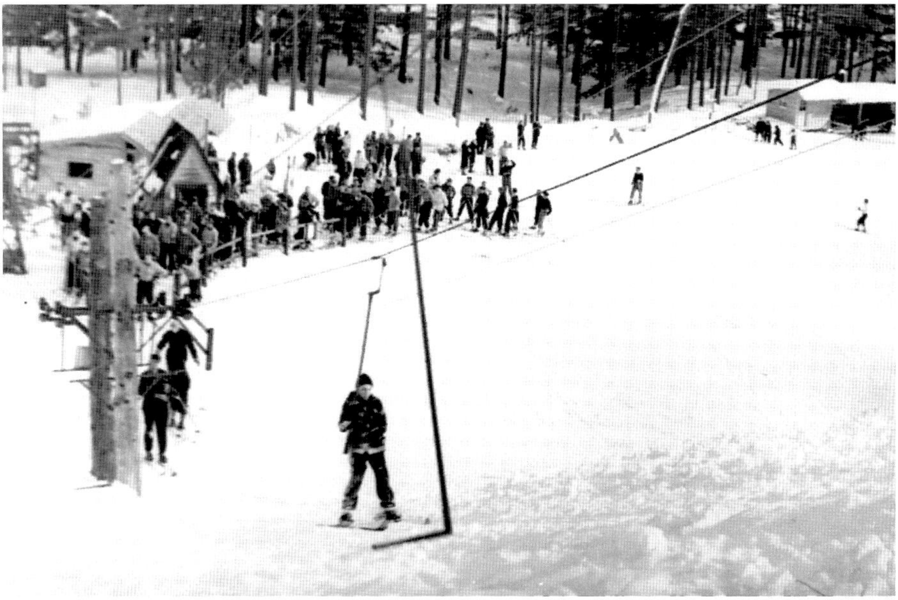

A large group of skiers line up to begin their ascent on the J-bar. In the distance, cars can be seen parked along Cooper Street. Skiers would have a short walk through the woods to reach Cobble Mountain. Route 87 slices directly through this location today, obliterating any trace of the lower portions of the ski area. *Courtesy of Mannix Publishing.*

> *then catch hold of the wooden arm and guide the horizontal bar to an appropriate location midway between the waist and the knees and do not sit down. You get a quick momentary boost, and then settle down to a very steady easy ride at the exact speed of 4.5 miles an hour (Per the management). A couple of weekends ago when we were there quite a few New York skiers ignored the advice of the management as to what to do with the horizontal bar. They either sat on it or placed it carefully in the small of the back, both maneuvers being equally and definitely unsuccessful…The last hundred or so feet at the top travel, for some obscure reason, over a little valley about 60 feet deep, so you should get off before you arrive over it. If you don't, the whole thing will be stopped by a safety gate anyway.*

A ski lodge was never constructed at Cobble Mountain. Instead, there was a "little tent [cabin] where you can get sandwiches and coffee but no place to get warm." A ski patrol took care of the slopes, filling in holes and stationing emergency equipment along the trails.

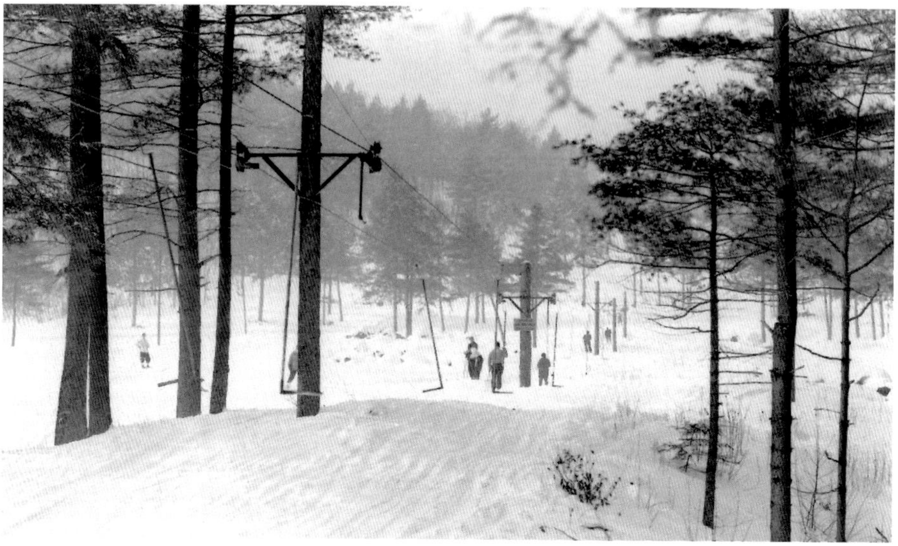

A view of the bottom of the J-bar and surrounding slopes. Note the gladed nature of the terrain and that one of the towers was a still-standing tree. The sign on the second tower reads, "Don't swing hangers when getting off." *Courtesy of Paul Imrie.*

Receipts for the first season were definitely on the low side. Just $238 was collected from the sale of tickets. The area was described as being fairly expensive, at $1.50 per day, when nearby rope tow areas typically charged $0.50 to $1.00 a day. Despite the low turnout for the first season, a reporter described the area as "worth visiting, not only for the quality of skiing but for the view of the lake and surrounding mountains."

By the second season, receipts were on the increase, generating nearly six times the income of the first season, with $1,223 collected. Ski races such as one sanctioned by the United States Eastern Amateur Ski Association (USEASA) were held in early 1939 with a combined downhill and slalom. Plans were developed to expand the ski slopes to the summit during this season, with some construction work completed before the area opened near New Year's Day. Some of these trails were finished by the 1939–40 season, including the Black Spruce Trail off Big Hollow Road and Milt's Trail, named after the former president of the ski club who had recently died. This trail started from the summit and ran down the west side of the mountain to the bottom of the ski tow and was intermediate in nature.

In addition to these improvements, a branch of Otto Schniebs's American Ski School out of Lake Placid taught lessons at Cobble Mountain. His

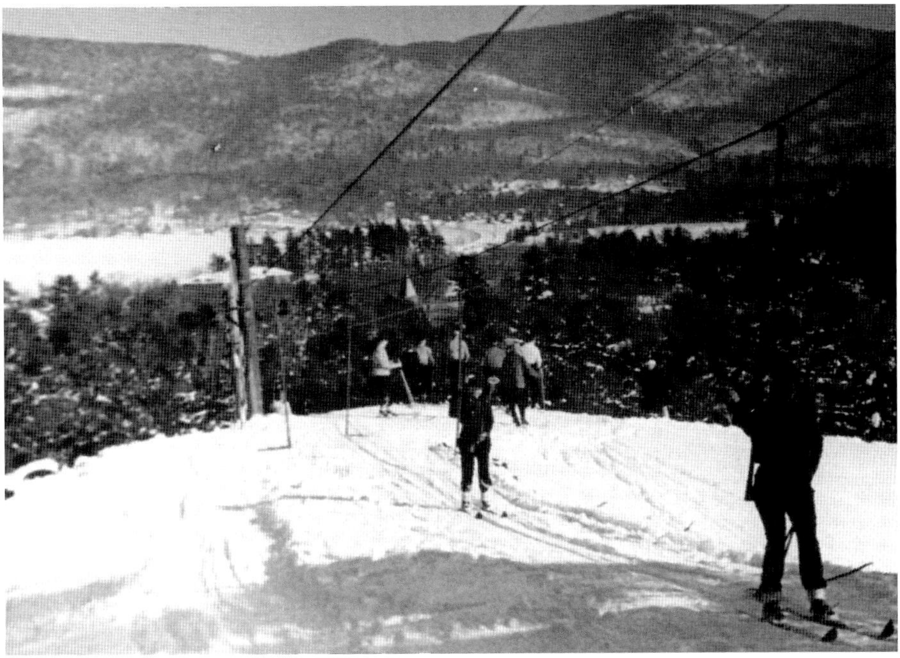

Skiers riding the upper portion of the J-bar had a spectacular view of Lake George. Below this knoll was a wide-open slope that led to the base of the ski area. *Courtesy of Mannix Publishing.*

ski school was the leading authority of instruction across much of the Adirondacks in the late 1930s and 1940s, with instructors at many areas. Vic Lefebrve also remembers that during this time, the use of skipjacks was prevalent on the slope. These are seats mounted on a single ski, which provided for an interesting way down.

Receipts for the 1939–40 season were the highest recorded for Cobble Mountain. At $1,651, they were still quite modest as compared to other Ski Tow Inc. areas such as Little Bromley and Intervale in New Hampshire.

The following season started off strong. The local chamber of commerce contracted Dolphus S. Cooper and Lyman Durkee to clear the slopes and ordered local manager Orson Schemerhorn to prepare the slopes for the new year. Receipts were down for this season to $794, less than half the previous season.

At the same time, Fred Pabst's growing ski area, Big Bromley, located just to the east of Manchester, Vermont, was showing an increase in growth. Combined with Little Bromley across the street, these two areas grossed nearly $6,000 in the 1940–41 season. Pabst saw the potential at Bromley and the lack of sales at Lake George. Owning a mountain with smoother slopes and much higher natural snowfalls, Pabst closed ski area operations at Lake George and Mount Aeolus, Vermont, and moved the valuable J-bars to Bromley. The Lake George lift became the upper J-bar at Bromley and operated for twenty years before being replaced by a modern double chairlift.

Thus, Lake George's unique ski lift, the only kind in New York State, came to end in 1941, but a small portion of the slope would make a brief return a few years later as a rope tow ski area.

Visiting the Area

Gaining access to the former Cobble Mountain ski area is somewhat difficult. Cooper Street, between Caldwell Avenue, Mohican Street and Interstate 87, was the location for the lowest portion of the slope, though houses are in this region now and the area was altered with the construction of the highway. Above this, more of the slope was developed into Interstate 87 from 1963 to 1964, obliterating the lower portions of the former ski area.

If you are driving north on Interstate 87, you can pass through the location of the former ski area approximately one-quarter mile south of the Prospect Mountain hiking bridge, but there is nothing to see from the highway, as the slope has been greatly modified.

You can also see the view from the top of the ski slope at the first turnoff on the Prospect Mountain Highway, though the slope has completely returned to forest. From the waters of Lake George itself, just offshore the village, the grown-in slope can just be distinguished on Prospect Mountain below the turnoff, though it takes a bit of imagination.

It is possible to hike in to the middle portions of the slope, but this is a difficult scramble due to a stream and is not recommended for the casual observer. In addition, there is little to see. Take the Prospect Mountain Hiking Trail across the pedestrian bridge over the Northway. Continue for a few hundred feet after crossing the highway to a power line. Turn left and scramble up the power line slope. Continue along the power line for about one thousand feet until you reach a stream. The easiest crossing is on the right, on the edge of the woods. Take extreme care in crossing the stream and climb up the other bank.

Once across, continue walking down the power line trail. You are now in the central part of the ski area. Uphill was the former wide-open slope, now forest. A small section of the J-bar lift line can be found downhill of the power line, which ends above the Northway (do not approach the highway!). Return the same way you arrived.

Cobble Slopes

Lake George, New York

Mid-1940s–circa 1950

After the original Cobble Mountain closed in 1941, the slopes remained empty for several years. Howard Macdonald, who had previously skied at the area, decided to reopen the area in the mid-1940s. He installed a rope tow, cleared the slopes and reactivated the area. He was assisted by Melvin Brown, who also had skied at the first incarnation of Cobble Mountain.

While not as large as the J-bar area, it offered a one-thousand-foot rope tow, a ski shop and affordable rates of a dollar and a half per day. Trails included the Cobble Slope, Top-of-the World and Roaring Brook; the first two were also lighted for night skiing. Vic Lefebvre remembers that the ski center's lower elevation and angle bathed it in sunlight, which led to frequent melting. Cobble Slopes closed around 1950 and never reopened.

Visiting the Area

Please see directions for Cobble Mountain if you wish to visit this area.

Top of the World

Lake George, New York

1938–41

Today, Top of the World, located high above Lake George on French Mountain, is a beautiful eighteen-hole golf resort with spectacular views of the Adirondacks and surrounding areas. It also once boasted a rope tow ski area in the late 1930s and early 1940s.

In the 1920s and early 1930s, Charles and Helene Tuttle purchased property surrounding the area with the goal of opening a resort. In 1936, they had finished acquiring land and built a lodge that had thirteen rooms and could sleep forty-five guests. Although the area was originally designed for summer tourists, it was evident to the owners that skiing could be a valuable amenity, and non-lift-served ski slopes and trails were added for the 1936–37 season.

Members of the Schenectady Wintersports Club were guests at Top of the World in January 1937. They described the lodge as being comfortable, with a kitchen that was "fast learning the extent of a skier's appetite." A large, open slope was available in front of the lodge, with runs up to a quarter of a mile long. Vehicles were available to hoist skiers back to the lodge so that more runs could be made in a day. For non-skiers, a large porch with chairs was available to take in the scenery, described as being "similar to the atmosphere of Switzerland or Austria."

More trails were available behind the lodge. In a January 8, 1937 report, the Wintersports Club noted:

> *Behind the lodge is a choice of four trails. Two of these are novice but interesting. A third is intermediate and the fourth is best. The lower part of the trail is wide but rather steep and straight. It was christened about three weeks ago when four of us ardently struggled down on three inches of snow among stumps and rocks which spitefully showed their tops above it.*

With the Wintersports Club displaying its approval of the facilities, plans were immediately made to build a rope tow for the following season. For the 1937–38 season, a rope tow was built just below the lodge on the open slope. A rustic ski jump was also constructed near the lodge.

For the first season of operation, the Tuttles wanted to make a splash with international guests. Birger and Sigmund Ruud, Norwegian Olympic ski jumpers, were brought in and performed various jumps and stunts for guests in early February 1938. Birger had won the gold medal in Lake Placid for individual large hill, while Sigmund had won silver in 1928 at St. Moritz. They performed quite the show, according to an article in the *Schenectady Gazette*:

> *As guests of the proprietors of Top o' the World lodge, the Ruuds came north from New York after returning from the west where they annexed*

> *several new honors in jumping. Shouldering the eight foot jumping skis they design and make themselves, they climbed the one hundred foot ski jump near the lodge and proceeded to astound the small crowd of spectators by leaping 118 to 120 feet. The leaps, of course, are not records but from the rustic jump, which is little more than eight or 10 feet high from the top of a small hill, they were considered amazing. Even on that small jump championship form was easily noticeable.*

Various other competitions were held at the Top of the World throughout the season, with many attendees and participants coming from the Schenectady Wintersports Club. Over the next few years, a Top of the World Club was formed to help promote and maintain the area. Its members were also involved in maintenance at the Cobble Mountain ski area.

Despite the efforts of the Tuttles, the Top of the World Club and the Schenectady Wintersports Club, all of which promoted the area, the outbreak of World War II would put an end to the rope tow. In 1944, the rope from the tow was listed for sale in the *Glens Falls Post Star* newspaper. It is not known where the tow and rope ended up.

Visiting the Area

Top of the World, while no longer offering ski facilities, continues to operate today. It features an eighteen-hole golf course, restaurant, bed-and-breakfast and farm. No remnants of the tow exist, but visitors can still see the magnificent view of Lake George from the facilities. For more information and directions, visit www.topoftheworldgolfresort.com.

Hammond's Tow

Lake George, New York

Circa 1950s–1960s

Hammond's Tow, also known as Hammond's Hill, was a small ski slope located behind Hammond's Motel in Lake George. The exact dates of operation are unknown, as this area did not appear in any contemporary literature. However, aerial photography from 1964 and memories of several skiers prove that Hammond's did exist.

Located off Bloody Pond Road, just east of the Magic Forest Amusement Park, was the former Hammond's Motel. Offering amenities such as a swimming pool and hiking trails, it also featured a rope tow and slope behind the hotel. The tow was used mostly by guests of the hotel, but local skiers from Lake George and Glens Falls enjoyed the tow as well. Night skiing was also available.

David Leeret, who grew up in Glens Falls, enjoyed the area with his family:

> *I grew up in Glens Falls and remember skiing at Hammond's Tow. I think we called it Hammond's Hill. It was about five miles from my home, and it had lights for night skiing. It had a rope tow that was a challenge at times and ruined more than one pair of mittens a season. It must have been in the early 1950s that my brother and I skied there. Our father would take us up after dinner and sometimes brought along some other kids from the neighborhood. There was a small building at the base of the hill which had a bar that served a limited menu of hot dogs, etc. and also served "adult beverages." I think that was the reason our dad was so anxious to take us skiing. The challenge was to see how many runs we could make and how fast we could ski down the hill.*

Jon Keating also skied here in the late 1950s:

> *As a kid I skied here, probably in the late '50s with wooden skis. There was some type of small storage area at the bottom, and it was very easy to fall off the tow, but it was a lot of fun. The tow was on the far left of the hill, and the hill was maybe three to four hundred yards of open field to the right. I cannot remember paying anything, but there must have been some charge.*

The area was almost certainly abandoned by the mid-1960s, though Hammond's Motel continued to operate into the 1990s. The ski slope gradually turned back into forest, and it is difficult to make out its location today.

Visiting the Area

Hammond's Tow is located on private property and is not publicly accessible, though the property can easily be seen on Bloody Pond Road. From the junction of Bloody Pond Road and Route 9, drive east one-third of a mile. The former motel is on the right, with the slope behind it the location of the former tow. As you can see, it has completely grown back in and is difficult to distinguish from the surrounding forest.

King George Motel

Lake George, New York

Circa 1960s

The King George Motel in Lake George was located at the present location of the Travelodge, just south of Exit 21 on I-87. Greg Schaefer remembers that his father, Carl Schaefer (who built the first rope tow in New York State), was hired by the owners to build an electric rope tow and design trails for guests behind the motel. He also remembers how his father had originally designed trails but found them bulldozed at the end of the project:

> *Dad was pretty good at laying out the trails so skiers would have a fun, interesting experience there. We arrived toward the end of the project, and the owner had pretty much bulldozed the hill into a straight run. Needless to say, Dad didn't like it, but the owner was probably erring on the side of safety. Dad also had a sign made using the Swiss ski poster model to advertise the tow.*

Greg's brother Chris recalls that the slope was floodlit and that the electric tow was much easier to use than previous gasoline engines; all it took was a flip of the switch and the tow was operational.

Otherwise, little else is known about this operation, as the motel no longer exists and it did not appear in ski listings, but it was almost certainly used solely for guests.

Visiting the Area

Nothing remains of this lost area, as the Travelodge (www.travelodgelakegeorge.com) is now located over the site. It is located just south of Exit 21 on Route 9, on a knoll overlooking Lake George.

STRAWBERRY HILL

Queensbury, New York

Early 1950s–54

Strawberry Hill, located on Bay Road in Queensbury, was in operation throughout the 1950s and was popular with Glens Falls locals. A true family area, it flew under the radar and was never mentioned in newspaper accounts or ski area guidebooks. It was operated by Mr. and Mrs. Claude Adams. The relocation of Bay Road in the fall of 1954 led to the partial removal of the hill, and skiing was discontinued.

Russ Murray, who grew up in Glens Falls, gives the following account of skiing at Strawberry Hill:

> *This "tow" was located on Bay Road to the north of Glens Falls between the city and Dunham's Bay on Lake George and was on Strawberry Hill. I learned to ski there in the early 1950s, along with many other Glens Falls youngsters. The hill was operated by the Adams family, and they were the instructors as well. I remember the parents only as Mr. and Mrs., but the son was Bruce. He was the first amputee skier that I had ever seen and was a great instructor for a group of kids. The talk was that he had been injured in the "war" (World War II or Korea) but I don't think anyone really asked. Mr. Adams would cruise through town early Saturday morning and we would throw ourselves and our gear into the back of a large black vehicle (no seatbelts—no seats!) for the short ride to the hill.*
>
> *Mornings were spent climbing the hill for the short ride down; herringbone for the "advanced" and sidestep for the beginners. Once the slope was thus "groomed" and we had our lunch, they would try (heavy on the "try") to fire up the old car at the top of the hill around whose left rear wheel was wrapped the rope for our tow. If the tow gods were kind and there was enough fuel, we had the lift for the afternoon.*

Visiting the Area

Strawberry Hill was sliced by the relocation of Bay Road, and the remainder of the hill is now covered in trees. It can still be viewed directly west, across the street, of the junction of Bay Road and Old Bay Road in Queensbury. No trace of the rope tow exists.

Kolan Family Tow

Queensbury, New York

1960s

Andy Kolan, who lived on Owen Avenue in Queensbury, used to operate a rope tow for family and neighborhood children in his backyard in the 1960s. This operation was never advertised and was simply one of a few truly backyard-type ski areas in the Adirondacks. The vertical drop was quite short, less than fifty feet, but the neighborhood children certainly enjoyed it.

Kathy Pennucci, who grew up on a neighboring street, remembers the tow fondly:

> *I lived on Lynnfield Drive in Queensbury from 1962 to 1967. One of our neighbors, Andy Kolan on Owen Avenue, had a rope tow in the backyard! All of the kids in the neighborhood spent every waking moment either sledding or skiing at the Kolans'. As I recall, it was even lighted for night skiing.*
>
> *If no one was outside when you got there, you just knocked on the door and handed the electric cord in through the window and Mrs. Kolan would plug it in for you. Can you imagine a whole neighborhood of kids using a rope tow, pretty much unsupervised, every day all winter? I don't remember anyone ever getting hurt, but no one would dare do this these days.*

The Kolan family has moved away from the area, and based on the author's visit to the area, it is believed that the slope has become reforested. New home and road construction surrounding Owen Avenue have also greatly changed the landscape.

Visiting the Area

Kolan's Tow is not publicly accessible and is on private property. The exact location is believed to be located just north of the junction of Lynnfield Avenue and Owen Avenue, but again, there is nothing to see.

Stone Mountain

Lake Luzerne, New York

Late 1930s–early 1940s, circa 1951–76

Stone Mountain Ski Area in Lake Luzerne was a long-lasting community ski area that would have probably survived a lot longer if not for persistent vandalism. It had a steep slope, several woods trails and a great view of the Hudson River.

The ski area was founded on property owned by Niagara Mohawk and Herman Roy and was started by Stuart Townsend. He was a physical education teacher at the Hadley-Luzerne Central School and believed that a community ski area would be a source of healthy exercise for the children. Students, teachers and community volunteers helped to clear the slope and build the rope tow, which operated in the late 1930s to the early 1940s. Townsend served in the navy and returned to Lake Luzerne in 1945. The ski area was let go for a period after World War II.

Around 1951, Stuart Townsend again started up the ski area at Stone Mountain. He founded the Stone Mountain Ski Club, which had nearly one hundred members at its peak around 1960. Townsend was now the supervising principal of the school and would later become superintendent. Two rope tows served the slope: a short beginner tow and a longer expert one. Plenty of children learned to ski at the area, and Townsend was one of its biggest supporters.

Stone Mountain gradually declined in usage in the 1960s and may have closed altogether for a short time in the latter half of the decade. The Lions Club then became involved; its motto is "We Serve," and having a community resource such as a ski area helped its goal. The ski area would serve youth by being a positive place for them exercise and have fun.

To prepare for the winter of 1969–70, the Lions Club worked extensively at the ski area. The former rope tow had been heavily vandalized and cut and needed to be replaced. New towers were put into place by Niagara Mohawk, arranged by Don Scribner. The rope was purchased from the Columbia Rope Company in Auburn, New York.

Lion Mike Berliner remembers that the hut was built to shelter the rope tow engine, along with a barrel where fires could be lit, warming the tow engine so it could operate. The fire would become "cherry red hot" and would keep both the tow and the operator toasty warm. Berliner recalls that

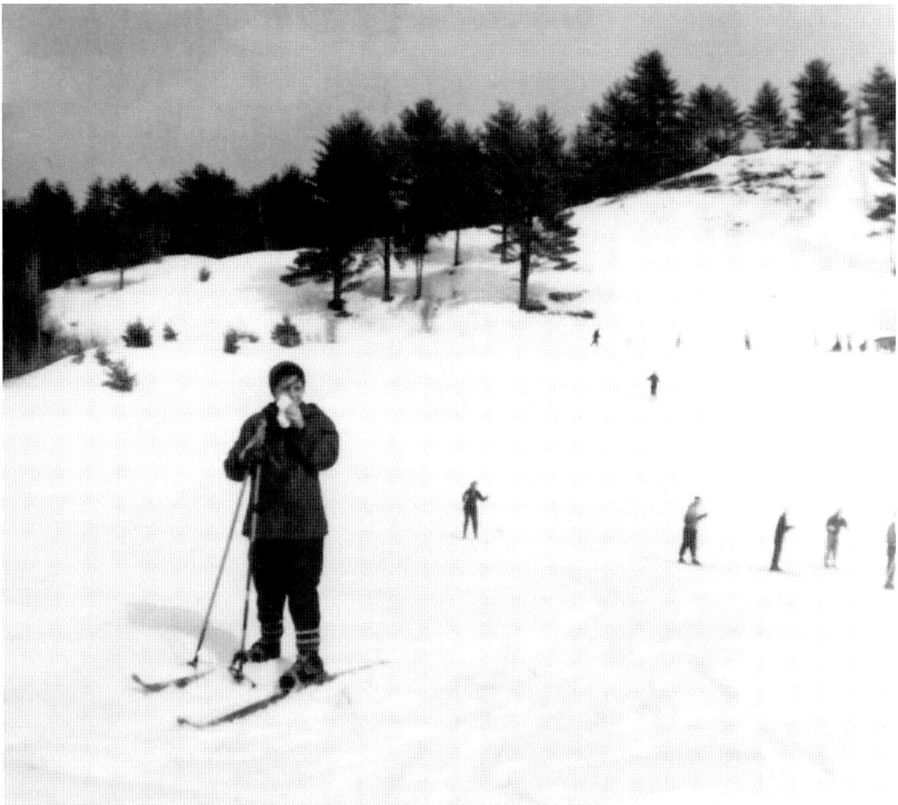

An undated but likely late 1950s view of Stone Mountain in Lake Luzerne shows the wide-open slope served by a rope tow on the right and additional gladed slopes to the left. Stuart Townsend, the principal of the school in town, was the founder and driving force during the early years of Stone Mountain. *Courtesy of Mary Joan Castle Kurimski, provided by Bea Evans.*

a shipping container obtained from the Port of Albany, where Lion John McGahay worked, served as a warming hut. Hot chocolate and refreshments were available. Another Lion volunteer was Walter Maxfield, who was also the president of the school board and spent countless hours at the tow, like many in the Lions.

In time, vandalism hit the ski area hard. The rope tow was shot at, the rope was cut and snowmobiles ruined the trails. The final straw occurred in 1976, when a vandal dumped sand into the engine of the tow, ruining it. The owner of the property, Herman Roy, offered to donate another engine, but the town could not guarantee its security, and the ski area was abandoned.

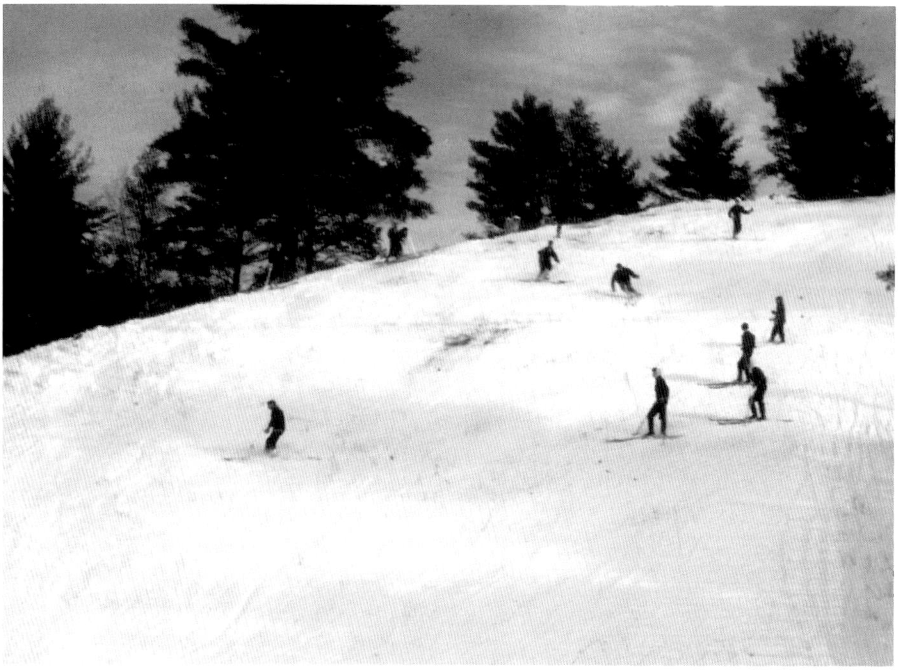

While short, Stone Mountain did have quite a pitch, as evidenced here in this close-up view from the 1950s. In later years, the town's Lions Club would assume operation of the ski area, but heavy vandalism by youths to the rope tow resulted in the area being abandoned in 1976. The greatest irony with Stone Mountain is that it was there to give young people a healthful and fun activity, yet it was destroyed by a small minority of them. *Courtesy of Mary Joan Castle Kurimski, provided by Bea Evans.*

Visiting the Area

Stone Mountain can be found on River Road in Lake Luzerne, 1.2 miles north of the junction of Main Street and River Road, on the right. You will see the heavily eroded steep slope a short distance from the road. Take caution exploring the area, and be on the lookout for any no trespassing signs. The rope tow has been removed.

Hull's Slope

Warrensburg, New York

1936–41, 1948

Hull's Slope, located off River Street in Warrensburg, was a classic early rope tow ski area. Conveniently located within walking distance of the downtown area, the tow was located on Howard Hull's farm. This tow was also one of the earliest in New York State and was installed during the fall of 1936.

Warrensburg was no exception to the rapid gain in skiing and outdoor winter sports across the Southern Adirondacks in the mid- to early 1930s. The Warrensburg Ski Club was founded on December 18, 1935, and sought to promote skiing in town. Henry O. Fassett of the American Legion had come up with the idea of founding this club. Gilbert Potter was elected as president, Bertram Whittemore as vice-president and Clifford Austin as secretary and treasurer. Roy Randall, Dr. John Cunningham, Lee Orton, John Musgrove and Mack Hall were elected to the executive committee. Orton would later become town supervisor and would work to open a rope tow on Blister Hill in the 1960s.

Although the ski club was made official just before winter, work rapidly progressed to offer some skiing terrain for that winter. The three-mile-long novice Big Brook Trail was carved out on Harrington Hill, and in January 1936, the intermediate one-and-a-half-mile-long Bald Knob Trail was cut from higher terrain on Harrington Hill Road to Hull's Farm. Automobiles could be driven to the start of these trails, which contained both uphill and downhill sections. Open slopes at the farm provided an ideal location for those practicing or learning how to ski. Having laid the initial foundation for ski facilities, the stage was then set to have a lift-served ski area.

The Warrensburg Ski Club began work on building a ski tow. Construction commenced in the fall of 1936, and a rope tow opened at Howard Hull's farm on Saturday, December 12, 1936. Three hundred feet in length, the tow gave skiers runs up to six hundred feet on either side of the tow. The ski area was managed by Clifford Hall during that first season. Hull graciously allowed the club to use his property without charge. There were some bugs to work out on the tow that first weekend, but the skiing was described as most enjoyable.

The goal of the ski club was not to rival North Creek or even Lake George (which at the time was developing into a brief but major ski center). Rather,

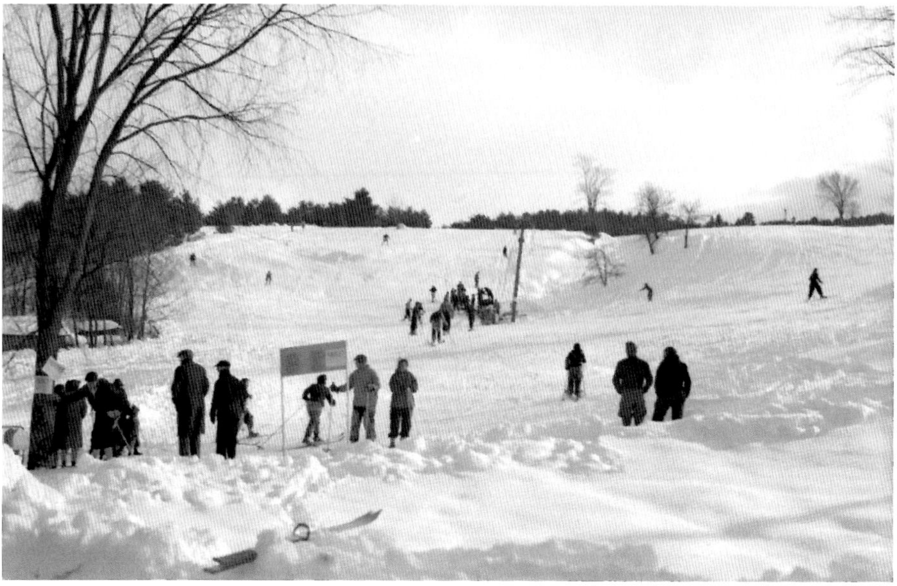

Hull's Slope in Warrensburg offered skiers a chance to enjoy an easy open slope with a three-hundred-foot-long rope tow. This view, likely from sometime in the 1936–38 timeframe, shows skiers enjoying the wide-open slope. Spectators are also seen at the base, likely enjoying the novelty of the rope tow. *Courtesy of the Warrensburgh Historical Society.*

the goal was to provide a local slope for local skiers without the need of having to drive on icy roads. Most skiers could even walk to Hull's Slope, as it was very close to town.

Hull's Slope gained in popularity throughout the late 1930s. In fact, special considerations had to be made for parking the numerous cars that would show up, as they sometimes blocked Hull's driveway. Articles were written in the *Warrensburg News* reminding skiers of appropriate behavior on the slope, including filling in sitzmarks, the indentations in the snow caused by falling skiers.

Informal slalom racing became popular at Hull's in the early 1940s. Children's races were held during the 1939–40 season, and on March 9, 1940, adults had the chance to race down the slope. The snow was wet and sticky, and the racing was difficult. Many crossed the finish line in "undignified positions, generally skis skyward, in a cloud of snow," according to the *Warrensburg News*. Race times were not published so as not to embarrass the adults, whose times had probably been beaten by children earlier in the season.

With the area becoming popular, a ski patrol was formed in December 1940, led by Ray Hayes. The ski patrol became associated with the National Ski Patrol and worked hard to become fully trained to its standards. Special pins for the Warrensburg Ski Club were sold in area stores to help raise money for the training. Further improvements to the ski area came that same month when 1,500-watt lights were installed by the New York Power and Light Corporation. Now, skiing could take place in the evening after school and work, and the slope would be quite visible from town. Skiing was available on weekends, as well as Tuesday through Thursday from 7:00 to 10:00 p.m. In addition, a new five-hundred-foot-long electric tow replaced the original gas-powered one. This increased skiing terrain, which was now divided into novice and experienced skiers.

World War II broke out just one season after all these major improvements were in place. Recreational skiing took a backseat due to rationing, and with many members of the ski club drafted, skiing at Hull's Slope came to an end for the duration of the war. The equipment was left in place but deteriorated from a lack of use. The slopes were kept clear, however, as the property was a working dairy farm.

After the war, one more attempt was made at reactivating skiing at Hull's. In October 1947, skiers and former members of the now disbanded Warrensburg Ski Club met to restart the club. In November, Aubrey Hull was elected the new president of the club. The newly reorganized club took control of the assets and liabilities of the original club and worked right away to open the slope for the rapidly approaching winter season. Much work had to be made on the tow due to its six years of idling, and numerous calls for volunteer labor were made through January 1948. Donations were solicited from area businesses and residents to contribute toward the reopening.

The tow finally opened in February, and lift-served skiing once again returned to Warrensburg. While briefly popular once again, new developments were now taking place nearby at Hickory Hill Ski Center. That area opened up at the same time as Hull's for the 1947–48 season, and it is surmised that the skiing at Hull's was not able to compete with the new development. Hull's closed for good in March, and on October 21, 1948, the Warrensburg Ski Club met to take up an offer to sell the tow to Hickory. This was agreed upon, the tow was removed and skiing came to an official end at Hull's. The final act of this incarnation of the ski club took place in February 1950, when the remaining assets of $9.70 were donated to the March of Dimes.

Visiting the Area

Hull's Slope is on private property but remains clear and easily viewed from River Road. There are no remnants of the tow since the lift was relocated to Hickory Hill Ski Center. From Exit 23 on Route I-87, turn west toward Route 9. Take a right turn onto Route 9, then take the second left onto Judd Bridge Road. At the end of Judd Bridge, where the road intersects with River Road, look up at the slope above you. That is the former location of Hull's Slope.

Blister Hill

Warrensburg, New York

1970–79

After Hull's Slope closed for good in 1948, twenty years would pass without an in-town ski area for Warrensburg. While Hickory Ski Center had opened for the 1947–48 season, it was too far to walk to from town. Community leaders and civic organizations, including the Kiwanis, saw the growth in skiing in the early 1960s and began to revisit the idea of having a nearby ski area that was aimed at children. It would be a project with great intentions and much hard work, but delays and various issues plagued the ski area from the start.

In January 1963, the Kiwanis Club started the process of opening a town ski area. John Hickey, who was the chairman of the Committee for Public Affairs of the Kiwanis, drafted a proposal to open a ski area. The chamber of commerce also supported the idea. The goal was to "provide a wholesome activity for teenagers, would be good for physical fitness, and would be a great training ground for the little ones."

In November 1963, a meeting was held to make a formal plan to open a ski center. A committee—led by John Hickey, as well as John Gould, Supervisor Lee Orton, Dr. C.E. Lawrence, D.D. Weaver, John Countryman, Donald Borth and Herrick "Hap" Osborne—met, and progress was made in developing a plan. The process was slow, however, and it was not until 1964 that a location on Hackensack Mountain in town was secured. The land was donated by Clara King Osborne and Julia King Willett.

Finally, in February 1965, trail locations were selected on Hackensack, as well as a six-hundred-foot lift line. A used seven-hundred-foot-long J-bar from a "nearby resort" (almost certainly from Alpine Meadows in South Corinth) was available. Discussions over whether to buy this J-bar or use a rope tow were debated, but in the end, a rope tow was selected. By this time, the Warrensburg Ski Club was involved in the plans. The future ski area was referred to as the Hackensack Tow.

In November 1965, the trails were cleared. The Jaycees were now involved as well, making this a real community effort. "Operation Brush Cut" was held on November 13, 1965, and was led by the volunteer effort of the Jaycees and the Warrensburg Ski Club to clear the slope. More plans were finalized to have the town's Park Department run the ski area, with ski patrol duties being split with the Warrensburg Ski Club. Rope for the tow was donated, and students from the vocational school reconditioned a gas engine.

During the following month, a flurry of activity took place at the ski area. Harold "Harry" Demarest, the president of the Warrensburg Ski Club, put out a notice that volunteers were needed every Saturday to continue to work on clearing the slopes.

Despite all of this work, it was not enough to open the ski center for the 1965–66 season; time just ran out before winter. A problem with a right of way access kept the area from opening in the 1966–67 season and even into the 1967–68 season. The rope tow was installed during this time, but it failed inspection. A warming hut was also built. Robert Frulla was another member of the Jaycees who was involved with the construction during this time period.

In the summer of 1968, vandals struck the area, damaging the motor. This occurred again in September 1968, when they cut the rope and damaged the lift house. Then, in March 1969, as the ski area was finally going to be turned over from the Jaycees and Kiwanis to the town, more vandalism struck. The rope tow was cut, signs were burned and shot at and the warming hut was trashed. This event certainly hit hard to all the volunteers who had worked on this project for more than half a decade, but they were undeterred and made the appropriate repairs.

On April 10, 1969, the Town of Warrensburg took official control of the ski area from the Jaycees and Kiwanis Club. It was during this time that the new name of the ski area was revealed to be Blister Hill, named by Maynard Baker, who had selected the best name in a contest. For this, he won ten dollars, which was promptly donated back to the Jaycees.

Now under the control of the town, Blister Hill finally opened to the public free of charge on Sunday, February 22, 1970. It had taken nearly six years of volunteer effort, with major setbacks due to vandalism and right of way issues, but it was finally open. Civic groups continued to volunteer at Blister Hill, with the Kiwanis providing free ski instruction.

From that first season until the 1978–79 ski season, Blister Hill provided a wonderful location for youths to ski for free in a safe environment. The wide-open slope with a vertical drop of about eighty feet was nonthreatening. Many fun winter events and junior races were held at Blister Hill.

Sadly, the last ski season was in 1979. Vandals hit the area hard later that year, burning the rope tow engine and destroying other facilities. This was the final straw for Blister Hill, and the area was never reopened. The burned-out lift engine was left at the top of the slope, which gradually became reforested for the next thirty years.

Like with Stone Mountain in nearby Lake Luzerne, vandalism, not weather or finances, led to the ski area's demise. Had the vandalism not taken place, there is a possibility that Blister Hill would still be open today, as other town-run ski areas, such as Dynamite Hill in Chestertown, are thriving once again.

Visiting the Area

Blister Hill, located on town land, still contains remnants of the former ski operation and can be explored freely. While the area was quite small, with only a short slope, recent logging operations and undergrowth can make hiking the area a bit tricky.

From the junction of Emerson Avenue and Route 9, Main Street (at the Grand Union Supermarket), turn right onto Emerson Avenue and then turn right onto Sunset Street. The entrance to the area is another tenth of a mile on the left; a gated dirt road leads to the area. There is parking for about one or two cars on the street near this entrance. Do not drive down the dirt road, and please be respectful of nearby homes.

Walk down the road for about three hundred feet until you reach a small clearing, used for logging during 2011. Turn left and walk up a trail that is briefly steep and then levels out to the summit after a few minutes. The engine for the rope tow remains at the top, still showing burn marks from the fire in the late 1970s.

The towline can be followed for about five hundred feet until you reach the bottom of the ski area. On the way down, notice the nearly completely reforested slope on your right, where hundreds of children learned the sport

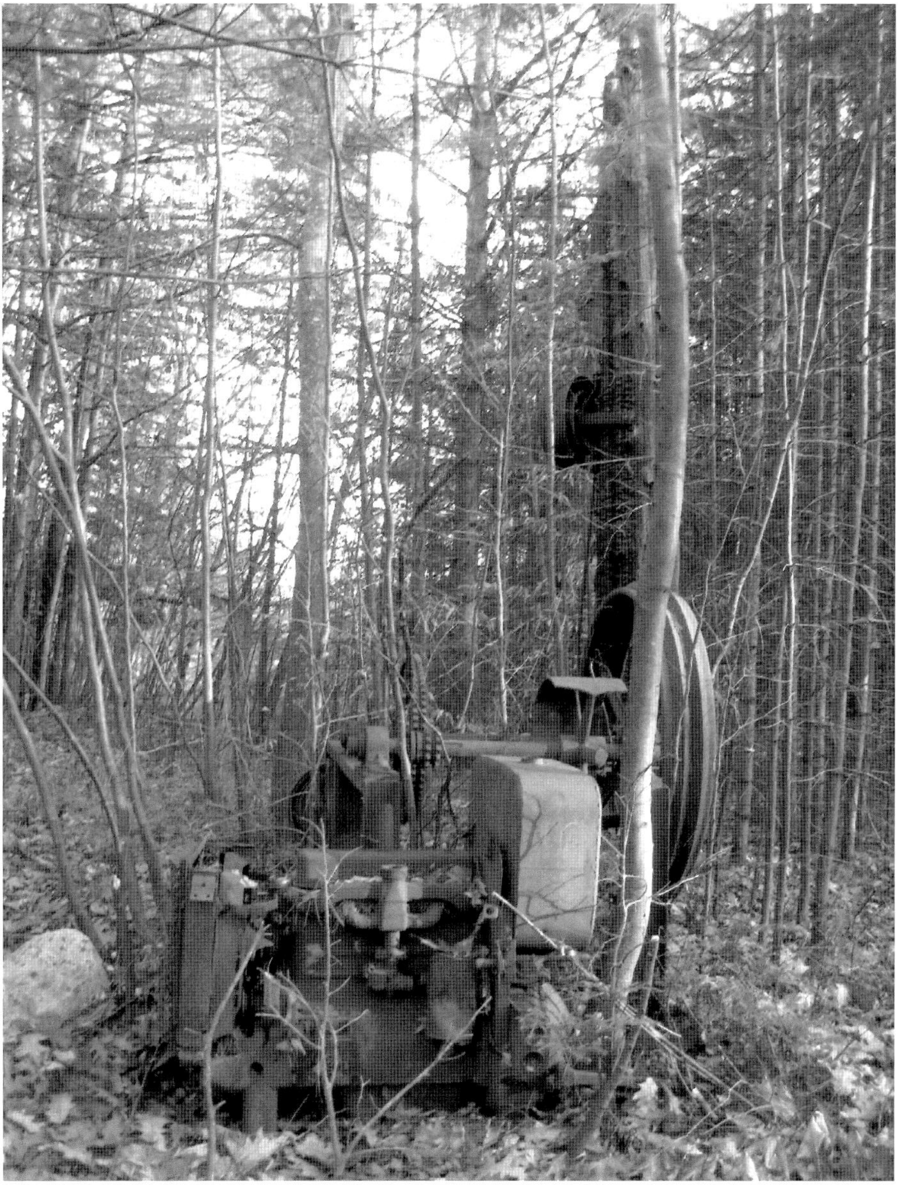

The burned-out remains of Blister Hill's rope tow remain at the summit of the lost ski area. The tow was torched by vandals in the late 1970s. As you can see below the engine, much of the former slope has been reforested. A few additional lift towers lying in the woods can be found by tracing the lift line to the base.

of skiing. On your left, note the occasional toppled towers on the left. Once at the bottom, portions of the old corral where skiers once lined up to ride the tow are visible, along with additional supports for the tow leaning against a pine tree.

From the base of the tow, turn right along the bottom of the ski area, and within a few hundred feet you will reach the clearing you saw when first entering the area. Exit the area on the same dirt road you entered.

FEDERAL HILL

Bolton Landing, New York

1946–47

Almost nothing is known about this short-lived rope tow in Bolton Landing. Only one reference in the *Warrensburg News* mentioned this area. During the 1946–47 ski season, a Mr. Connerty operated a rope tow "at the top of Federal Hill." He provided free skiing to high school students during a weekend in March. As there are no other sources on this area, it is believed to have operated only during that winter.

Visiting the Area

Due to the vague location "at the top of Federal Hill," an exact spot for this area could not be determined.

SAGAMORE HOTEL

Bolton Landing, New York

1949–51

A very brief operation, in 1949 the Sagamore Hotel in Bolton Landing operated a six-hundred-foot-long rope tow on the grounds of the hotel, along with a toboggan chute. According to contemporary accounts, the tow was obtained from North Creek and was installed with assistance from the

State of New York. It was the first time the hotel was open for winter sports. The slope could not have had more than a fifty-foot vertical drop, as the hotel is located on an island in Lake George. Listings for this tow continued to appear as late as 1951. It is believed that that the Sagamore ceased winter operations, thus closing the tow.

Visiting the Area
The Sagamore Hotel (www.thesagamore.com) is located on a private island and is open to guests and patrons only. It is believed that the tow was located on a wide lawn that faces the lake. No remnants of the tow or ski operation are visible.

Beech Hill

Schroon Lake, New York

1947–51

Skiing in the Schroon Lake area goes back well before lift-served skiing was introduced at Beech Hill. A Norwegian immigrant, Doc Suhrland, owned a local drugstore and was also an active cross-country skier. He made his own skis for family and friends and used belts from the defunct Ed Richardson's sawmill for crude bindings. Doc taught his children and locals, including Moe Friedman, who remembered learning how to cross-country ski at the town's golf course in the late 1920s and early 1930s.

By the mid-1930s, local skiers including the Suhrlands, Moe Friedman, Marion Hinds, Charles Hinds, Chet Cole, Buster Jenks, Charlie and Marabelle Woods, Dwinal Kerst and others ventured over to the rope tow developments in North Creek and became hooked on downhill skiing. After returning from visits to North Creek, the group decided to build a ski trail in town in 1936. Permission was obtained from landowners, and a nearly four-mile trail was constructed from Beech Hill west of town to the golf course, exiting near the fourth fairway. Moe Friedman remembers that a call was put out to volunteers, with a great response. However, the brush was cut at about six inches above the ground, and once the snow was packed, the trail became dangerous. This was remedied the following year.

The trail was popular for about three years before skiers moved on to other areas, as the trail was too flat as compared with the steeper trails in the North Creek region. It was abandoned by 1941.

Plans for a downhill, lift-served ski area in the Schroon Lake area began in 1941, when the Schroon Lake Ski Club was reorganized and attempted to construct a rope tow. A committee was set up in November 1941 to purchase a rope tow and find a property suitable for skiing. Dr. Booth, a local physician, led the effort. A tow was purchased in early December for $300, and an agreement was met with the McMillans to use their land for a ski area on the east side of Severance Mountain. A slope was cleared in December 1941, and volunteers were asked to help remove stumps to make the slope suitable for skiing. However, this is about all the progress that took place before the outbreak of World War II put a stop to any ski development until 1946. Dr. Booth served in the war and died in the service.

After the end of the war, ski area development resumed across New York, and in September 1946, the chamber of commerce in Schroon Lake studied the possibility of finally getting a ski tow in operation. Charles Hinds, the president of the chamber, held a meeting on September 19, 1946, at which Chester Cole told the members that a suitable location for a ski tow had been established on Beech Hill; $200 was appropriated for the project.

By October, the town board of Schroon itself had become involved, and a $2,000 budget for the construction and operation of the tow was approved. Half the money was obtained through a state grant through the Youth Commission, which was promoting healthy outdoor activities for children. The other half was from the chamber of commerce and $800 from the town budget. Part of the stipulation of the funding was that there would be no charge for youth to enjoy the facilities.

Once approved, development moved swiftly. Property on Beech Hill owned by the late Mike Ford was cleared. In late October 1946, Richard Moody, Charles Wood and Charles Hinds, along with local high school students, enthusiastically cleared the slopes, and on November 2, a general call to all locals was put out to help work on the area.

The need to purchase the ski tow was apparent, and instead of building a new lift from scratch, one was purchased from Ticonderoga at a "very reasonable figure." This was one of the two tows that served in the Punch Bowl area prior to World War II, though it is unknown which tow in particular was bought. Harold Swan, the town highway superintendent, and his crew picked up the tow on November 4.

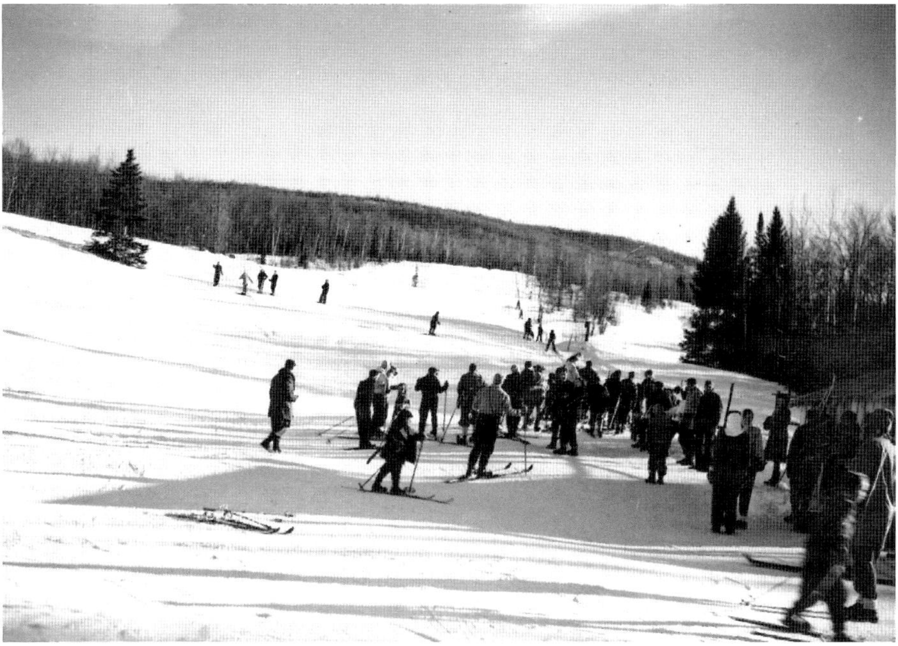

Skiers line up at the bottom of the rope tow at Beech Hill. A wide slope with scattered trees allowed more open skiing to the left of the tow, with a narrower trail found to the right. The slope had a vertical descent of 150 feet. *Courtesy of the Friedman family.*

On November 17, Charles Hinds, Chester Cole, Pete McMullen and Mel Darrow installed the engine for the tow. Hinds's father-in-law noted that skiers would "rave about the slopes, trails and the view!" Peter Pitkin helped deliver the poles for the lift, and members of the highway department helped finish up the tow by the end of the month.

Now, all that was needed was some snow. December produced little in the way of natural snowfall, though a one-inch accumulation did allow Charles Hinds a chance to test drive the slope on what must have been very sketchy conditions. Finally, enough snow allowed the area to open on January 1, 1947, as "a School bus took a crowded but merry group of students to the tow and therefore many children for the first time of their lives experienced the thrill of the tow and oh hum, coming down part way on skis." Buses were needed to transport skiers to Beech Hill, as it was too far to walk for almost all residents. In fact, the location just far enough outside of town on icy roads led to its downfall in 1951.

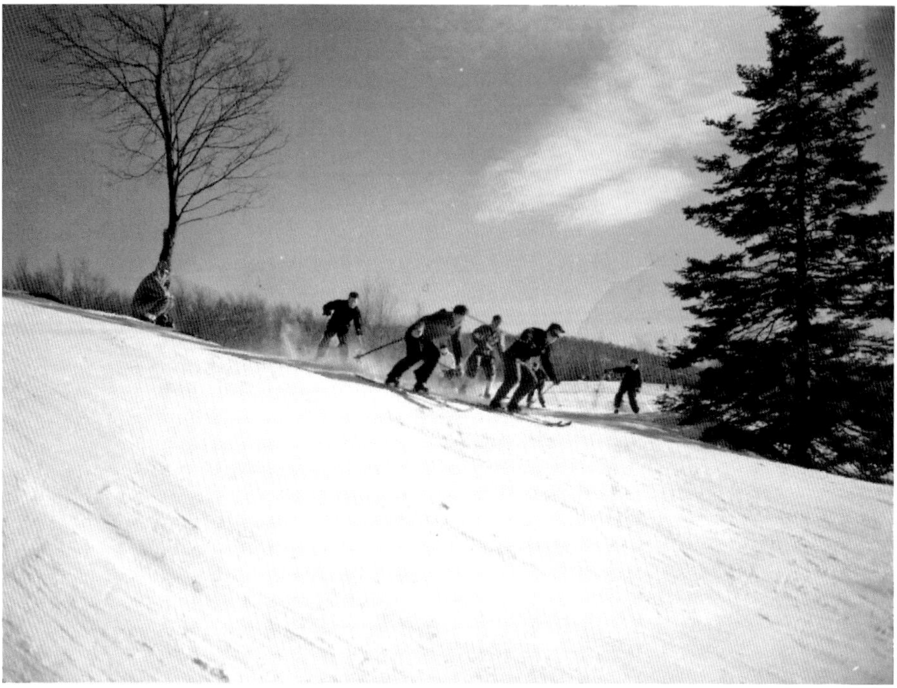

A group of racers flies down the open slope at Beech Hill, passing between two trees. Beech Hill was very popular with local children, and as many as one hundred could be found enjoying the slopes on a busy weekend. *Courtesy of the Friedman family.*

News traveled fast about this new area, and Otto Schniebs taught a few classes here in February and March 1947. It is amazing to think that such a small, local area would have a nationally famous instructor teaching ski school in the 1940s, but Schniebs enjoyed teaching skiing, and the slope at Beech Hill was perfect for this.

The first season came to end in March 1947. The second season would be delayed in nearly the same fashion as the first, opening on December 27, 1947. A series of rainstorms kept the area from opening again until early February 1948, when the Boy Scouts held a winter carnival. A new warming hut was constructed for that season, and Moe Friedman remembers that "there would be a hundred or more kids and adults on a busy weekend." Other skiers, including Joanne Treffs and her brother David, recall that "the area was the first they skied that had a rope tow and lodge, where you could warm up and buy hot chocolate."

The 1948–49 season had a very late start as well, and the tow did not open until Saturday, February 5. Due to all these late starts and the frequently icy and narrow road to the ski area, plans were made to move the tow to a closer location to town. Chester Cole, then president of the Schroon Lake Ski Club, proposed moving the tow to the golf course in town in December 1950. However, this was not to be, and the rope tow at Beech Hill ceased operations at the end of the 1950–51 season.

Cole was on the right track about opening a ski tow at the golf course. However, it would be another twenty-seven years before a Pomalift was constructed adjacent to the golf course. That story is told in the "Restored Ski Areas" chapter.

Although now lost, the area is still fondly remembered by skiers who enjoyed it, such as Betty Organek:

> *I remember having a great deal of fun at the Beech Hill Ski Area. A local school bus would come on Saturday and Sunday mornings and park outside of Friedman's. The kids would bring their ski equipment and load it in the back of the bus and we would go to Beech Hill. The bus would let us off at Hoffman Road and the entrance of Beech Hill, and we would carry our skis or ski out to the main area, which was a quarter of a mile. When we reached the area, we would put on our skis and go up the rope tow to the top of the hill. There were at least four trails, three of them easy and one of them more difficult.*
>
> *At the bottom there was a shack where we would gather either when we had enough skiing, needed a break or were cold. I remember having hot dogs and soda and playing cards and getting warm.*
>
> *The great thing about the ski area was that many members of the community, including kids and adults, would take advantage of it. Many schoolteachers would ski there as well.*

Visiting the Area

Virtually nothing is left of the former Beech Hill ski area. Homes have been built on the former slopes and trails, as well as new roads. Whatever has not been developed has returned to nature and become reforested. No remnants of the tow exist. The area can be reached by starting from the golf course and driving four miles west on Hoffman Road, then turning left onto Beech Hill Road. As you drive up Beech Hill Road, the former ski area was on the left, where woods and homes are now found. After about five hundred feet, turn left at the junction where Ski Tow Road bears left and away from the former area. You will then drive through the former slope just east of the junction. As the lost area is now private property, please do not trespass.

The Punch Bowl

Ticonderoga, New York

1938–43

While brief in operation, the Punch Bowl complex in Ticonderoga was a unique ski train destination in the late 1930s. Operating in the historic Lord Howe Valley, this complex of nine trails, two rope tows, a toboggan chute and a clubhouse made the ski center one of the largest in the Southern Adirondacks. Its low elevation and southeast exposure led to a lack of consistent snow depth and its eventual demise.

Throughout the winter of 1935–36, ski enthusiasts in Ticonderoga began the process of organizing into a ski club. They undoubtedly had learned of the tremendous development taking place to the west in North Creek and wanted to capitalize on the surge of skiing. In early February 1936, a meeting took place that resulted in the formation of the Ticonderoga Snow Club. Its goal was to develop a winter sports resort in the Ticonderoga vicinity. Dues were only one dollar, and calls were made to all residents and businesses to join and support the effort.

After formation, the next matter of business for the club was to locate a suitable spot for development. Land between Route 9N and Three Brothers Mountain, later referred to on trail maps as the Punch Bowl, was selected. Trails were carved on Three Brothers and were named after the major players at Fort Ticonderoga. Names included Arnolds Revenge (named after Benedict Arnold) and Allens Surprise (named after Ethan Allen). A clubhouse and toboggan chute were also built. Slopes behind the clubhouse and Three Brothers were cleared to provide for wide-open skiing.

Club members had assistance in building these facilities. Members of the National Youth Administration (NYA), a Depression-era WPA group, helped provide labor for construction of the ski trails. Made up of young people ages eighteen to twenty-six, NYA members were paid thirty-eight and a half cents per hour of work, up to twenty hours every two weeks. The

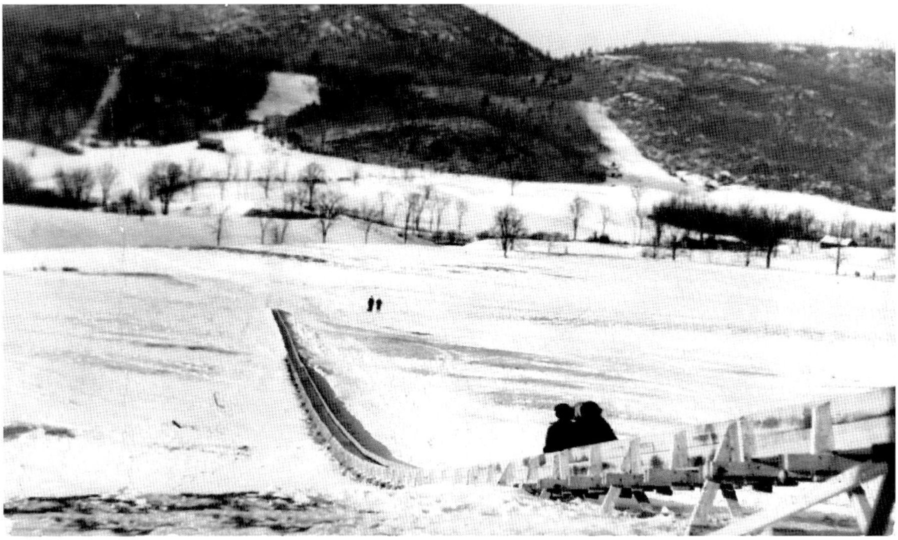

In addition to offering skiers two rope tows, a few wide-open slopes and trails, tobogganing was a popular attraction at the Punch Bowl. Appealing to skiers and non-skiers alike, the exciting toboggan run featured a view of the ski trails above. From left to right on the mountain is the main rope tow, Hill "36" and Pine Run. The clubhouse and the beginner tow on the Shattuck Slope are located beyond this photograph to the left. *Courtesy of the Ticonderoga Historical Society, Hancock House.*

NYA provided employment for local unemployed youths, providing much-needed income.

By October 1936, the majority of trail work was finished. On October 17, the facilities were shown to the public for the first time. A hike of the ski trails was enjoyed, and a contest for the best photograph of the slopes was held. Skiers would have to do without a ski lift for the next season, but many were accustomed to having to climb for their turns.

All the facility needed was snow. The timing could not have been worse for the opening of the Punch Bowl, as the 1936–37 ski season was a disaster. The ground was bare as of January, and what little snow did fall melted quickly. Snow trains from Schenectady and New York were cancelled, and little if any activity took place at the area.

Despite the lousy season, additional plans were quickly made for the following year. Fred Pabst Jr., of the Pabst brewing family, was opening lift-served ski areas throughout the United States and Canada. He operated Hill 70 in Quebec, Mount Aelous in Vermont and Intervale and Huckins Hill in New Hampshire. Additional lifts were built for the 1937–38 season,

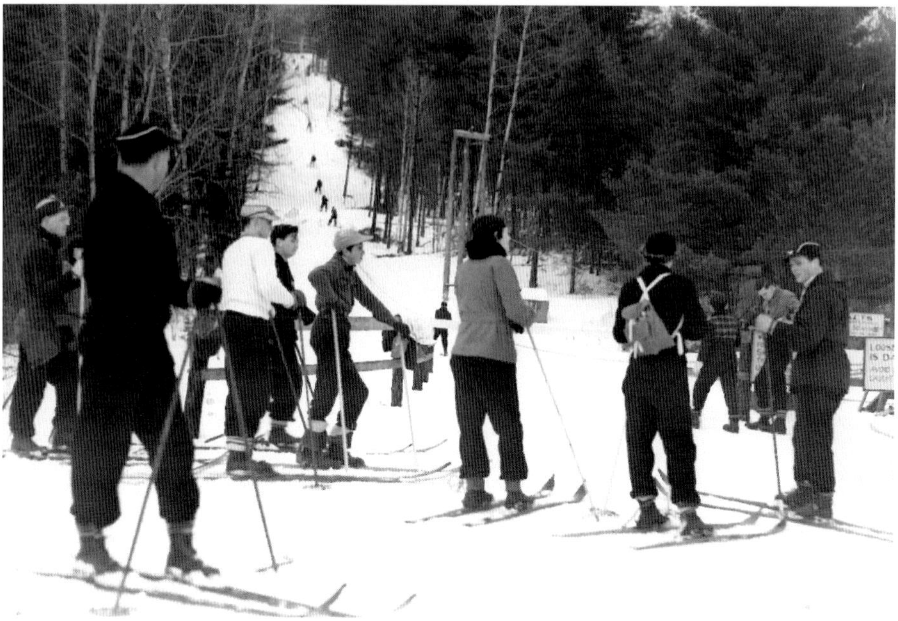

Skiers gather at the start of the upper rope tow in the Punch Bowl. Signs warned skiers not to have any loose clothing become entangled with the twisting rope, as dire consequences would result. The tow served Hill "36," the Lord Howe Slalom Run, a wide-open slope as well as Pine Run, an intermediate slope located farther to the north. *Courtesy of the Ticonderoga Historical Society, Hancock House.*

including at Lake George. He set his eyes on the facilities at Ticonderoga and worked out a lease with the snow club to open a rope tow. Built in 1937, this tow was quite long at 1,700 feet and was built to serve the lower slopes, including Hill 36 and Pine Run.

With the improvements to the facilities, Ticonderoga was poised to become a major ski center. Several snow trains were arranged for the first months of 1938, but a lack of ticket sales led to the cancellation of one from New York City in early January. The Schenectady Wintersports Club had reserved a train for January 23, which would be the first snow train in Ticonderoga.

On the weekend of January 15 and 16, members of the Schenectady Wintersports Club were guests of the Ticonderoga Snow Club and were treated to a preview of the center. The trails were described as being shorter in length than those at North Creek, and the expert trails were declared to be just as difficult. The Pine Run slope, served by the rope tow, was described as being aimed toward intermediates with a long run out. Hill

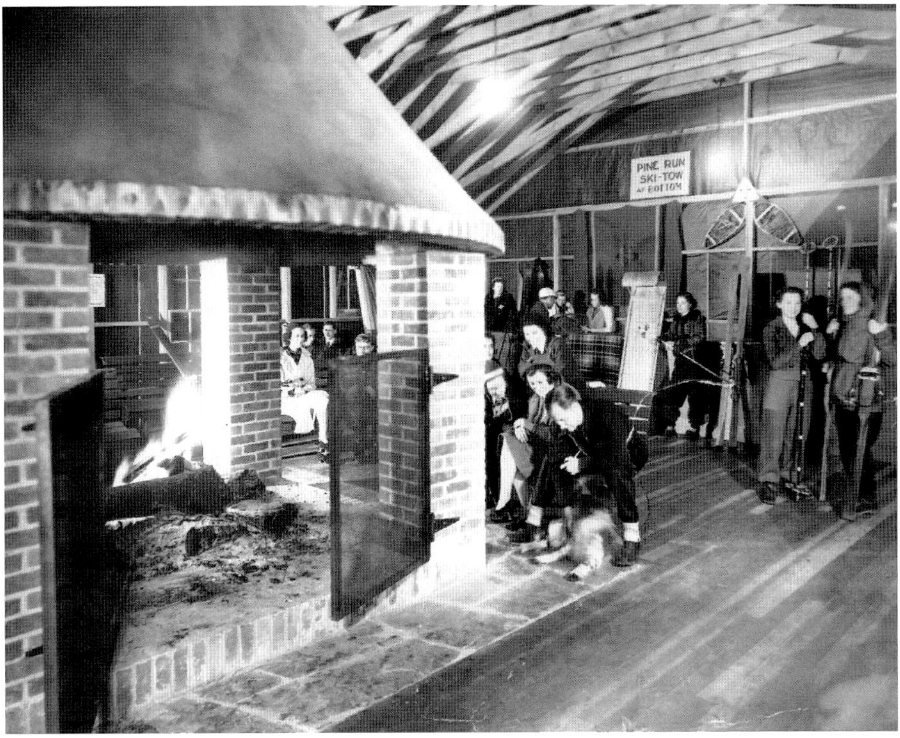

The interior of the Ticonderoga Snow Club's lodge provided a cozy spot for skiers to warm up between runs. Note the sign for the Pine Run Slope and tow posted on the wall. Although this building no longer stands, the metal hood above the large fireplace can still be seen from Route 9N today. *Courtesy of the Ticonderoga Historical Society, Hancock House.*

36, a more difficult slope, resembled "a landing like a ski jump." Finally, the clubhouse, which offered up coffee and sandwiches, had a "very novel fireplace" and allowed parents of younger skiers to watch them carefully from the bottom. In anticipation of the next week's snow train, a half-page spread filled with details on the trails and tickets was published in the *Schenectady Gazette*.

On Sunday, January 23, 1938, skiers gathered at Union Station in Schenectady and boarded the Delaware and Hudson Train for Ticonderoga. At 8:00 a.m., the train departed with eleven cars full of skiers and their gear. Around 10:30 a.m., they arrived in Ticonderoga. A total of 648 skiers, most members of the Schenectady Wintersports Club, disembarked and jammed the streets of Ticonderoga. This was what the town had been waiting for. Nearly the entire population greeted the skiers,

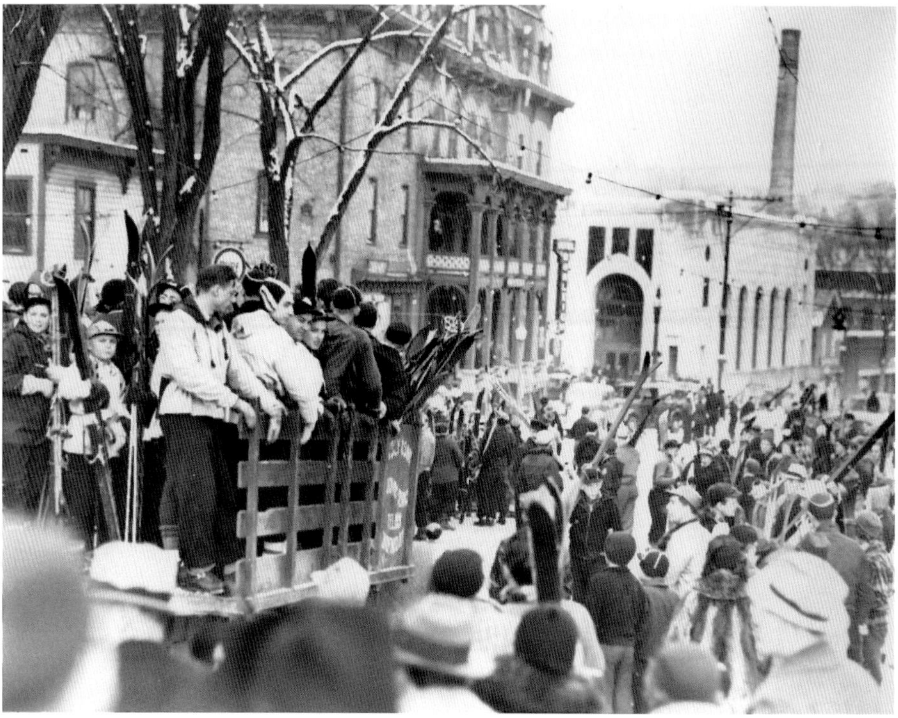

A throng of skiers fills the streets of downtown Ticonderoga after disembarking from the ski train in the late 1930s. Local residents and businesses provided any kind of transportation available for the five- to ten-minute drive to the slopes, including packing skiers in on truck beds. *Courtesy of the Ticonderoga Historical Society, Hancock House.*

and every method of transportation was utilized to take them the several miles to the Punch Bowl.

Unfortunately, the weather was not ideal for skiing. Temperatures were mild and the snow was sticky, but a good time was had by all. One skier, "Fran" Francis, performed jumps and tricks throughout the day and was a subject of many a camera lens. He also stood out in his attire, described as "being clad in a green flannel sport coat, fawn colored baggy knickers, dark stockings, black boots, and brilliant yellow sweater…this was topped off with a green Tyrolian hat of green in which a long brown feather was jauntily set."

Throughout the day, shuttles ran from the slopes to Ticonderoga as skiers lunched at various restaurants, supporting the local economy. After a long day of skiing, skiers returned to the station, and the train left at 6:00 p.m.

On the ride back, some skiers slept, while others danced away the trip to the Big Apple, a dancing craze at the time. Arriving back in Schenectady at 8:30 p.m., many skiers were exhausted but in terrific spirits. The tow brought in $114 to Ski Tows Inc., a sizeable sum of money in the midst of the Depression, equivalent to nearly $850 today.

This would be one of the few bright spots for the 1937–38 season. A lack of natural snowfall for the second season in a row led to little skiing for the rest of the winter, as only another thirty-four dollars in income was reported. This likely took place the weekend after the Schenectady snow train on January 30, when ski races and lessons by Otto Schniebs were held. Schniebs presented an illustrated lecture later that night at the high school gymnasium, where nearly three hundred residents were mesmerized by his presentation.

The low elevation and southeast exposure of the Punch Bowl area certainly did not help with natural snowfall. Fred Pabst made the decision to concentrate his efforts elsewhere and sold the tow to the snow club for $675 in November 1938.

Despite the second bad season in a row, another rope tow was constructed for the following year. This tow was a beginner tow and was located between the clubhouse and Route 9N, on the Shattuck Slope. Lights were installed for night skiing on the open slopes, and the toboggan chute was also floodlit.

The 1938–39 season would be much kinder to the Punch Bowl than previous years. A Schenectady Wintersports Club train brought 250 skiers on February 5, 1939, and on February 11, more than 500 skiers from New York City arrived on another snow train.

The following two seasons would also suffer from a lack of snowfall, with the tows operating sporadically. Snow trains were cancelled for both seasons, frustrating many who had promoted the ski area. The 1941–42 season would begin with the breakout of World War II, and thus skiing was limited as young men were being drafted. The rope tows did operate occasionally in early 1942 and again in 1943. Wartime restrictions at the Punch Bowl meant only weekend operation, and no cars were permitted to drive there due to gasoline rationing. Some buses were permitted to bring skiers to the slopes.

A combination of World War II restrictions, a lack of snowfall and frequently cancelled snow trains all factored in to ceasing operations at the Punch Bowl at the end of the 1942–43 ski season, and the ski facility was abandoned. Voters chose to lease the property and clubhouse to the Ticonderoga Fish and Game Club in November 1945, and the tow was sold in 1946 to Schroon Lake, where it began life anew at the Beech Hill

Ski Area. A few skiers continued to use the slopes on a non-lift-served basis throughout the 1940s, but soon after, many of the trails and slopes filled with tree growth. Today, barely any evidence of the complex on Three Brothers can be seen.

Visiting the Area

The Punch Bowl is located on private property; however, you can view the entire complex easily on Route 9N. From the Hancock House in Ticonderoga, head west on Hague Road (9N) for 1.4 miles. Park on the right shoulder, just past a curve. Looking to the west and northwest, you will see the Three Brothers and long slope that descends to the valley floor. Here was the location of Pine Run and Hill 36, as well as the rope tow. The slopes and ski tow have completely grown in, and it would take a keen eye to even spot where they were once located.

Directly below Route 9N is another slope, this one still clear. Here was the location of the toboggan run and Shattuck Slope rope tow. If you look closely below this slope in the underbrush, you can make out the large metal hood that was once above the fireplace in the clubhouse. The hood is the last remnant of the Punch Bowl development.

Chapter 3

LOST SKI AREAS OF THE SACANDAGA LAKE–FOOTHILLS REGION

The Sacandaga Lake and Foothills region of the Southern Adirondacks contain a wide variety of lost ski areas. A mixture of ski club hills, community areas and large mountains can all be found in the area. No snow trains visited these areas, which were mainly accessible via good state roads or were otherwise enjoyed mostly by local residents. Eleven ski areas have been lost in this region.

In the eastern section, the largest lost ski area in this book, and one of the best known, was located in South Corinth. Called Alpine Meadows and the Adirondack Ski Center, it was well known for having New York State's largest open slope and for myriad rope tows. Later, higher-capacity T-bars replaced the rope tows and extended the vertical drop to nearly one thousand feet. A property dispute led to its downfall.

Another significant ski area was Pine Ridge in Salisbury Center. Here, two unique parallel J-bars brought skiers to the top, where several trails and open slopes were available for a descent. This area benefited from both lake effect snows and nor'easters, which led to a lengthy season.

Several club-operated ski areas, like the brief Northville Winter Sports Club and the longer-lasting Indian Hill in Barneveld, allowed members to enjoy their own ski area. A community ski area, Little Alpine in Remsen, allowed local children the chance to ski for free.

MERTON'S HILL

Corinth, New York

1938–early 1950s

Founded by Jim Doherty and Fred Michaud, this ski area in Corinth was inspired by the two friends' visit to North Creek in the mid-1930s. Seeing the large ski development there, they decided to build their own rope tow closer to home to be used mainly by family and friends. The Merton Hill Ski Club was formed, with dues set at two dollars to provide for operating expenses.

The first tow was built in 1938, using an old Dodge truck Doherty and Michaud obtained in the town of Day. Their employer, the International Paper Company in Corinth, gave them old rope to use for the tow. This rope was too thick, and they had to order a thinner rope, which ended up working out just fine. Around 1940, the original Dodge truck was replaced by a Ford that was bought in Ballston Spa.

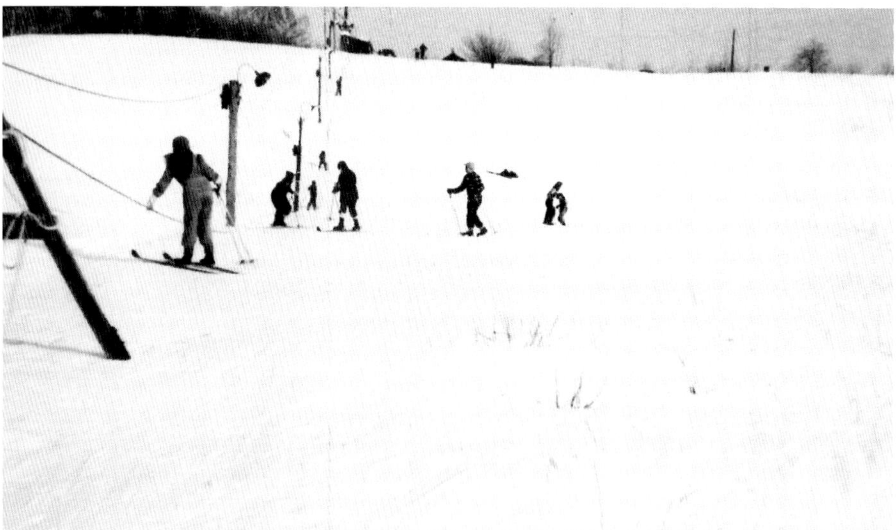

Merton's Hill in Corinth was a classic small ski area. A five-hundred-foot-long rope tow accessed about one hundred vertical feet of skiing on a wide-open slope. The tow was powered by an old Dodge truck that was purchased near Day, New York. The slope remains fairly open today but is located on private property below Paris Avenue. *Courtesy of the Kingsley family.*

With the outbreak of World War II, the ski area briefly closed, and the Ford was used as a tow truck in Corinth during this time. After the war, new operators—first Matt Mosher and then Donald Kingsley—operated the area throughout the rest of the 1940s. A ski hut was built by Kingsley in 1947 and was later moved to Kingsley's property in Corinth, where it is now used as a storage shed. Night skiing was also available at Merton's Hill.

The ski area gradually faded away in the early 1950s, though the slope was still used for sledding until the 1960s.

Visiting the Area

Merton's Hill is located on private property behind homes on Paris Avenue in Corinth and is not accessible. The slope remains somewhat clear, but no remnants of the rope tow remain in place.

Sisto's Slope

South Corinth, New York

1936–38

Sisto's Slope, located in South Corinth, was developed by the Saratoga Ski Club in the mid-1930s. It operated for a few years with a rope tow until a property dispute shut it down. In the mid-1940s, this general area was developed into Alpine Meadows, one of the longest-lasting and biggest ski areas to become lost in the Southern Adirondacks.

The Saratoga Ski Club was founded in 1935 and sought to open up some ski terrain closer to the city. A suitable location in South Corinth was secured at the Sisto Farm at the foot of the Kayaderosseras Range. A novice trail, the Sisto, was cleared and was three-quarters of a mile long, ending in slalom slope. For the 1935–36 season, no lift was available, but skiers enjoyed the slopes. A slalom featuring Union, Dartmouth and Saratoga Ski Teams was held in January 1936. In addition, more trails were cleared on the Kayaderosseras Range nearby, including the Moody and Juniper Trails.

A rope tow was built and operated at Sisto's for the 1936–37 season, as well as the 1937–38 season. Ed Taylor, who operated Taylor's Sport Shop in

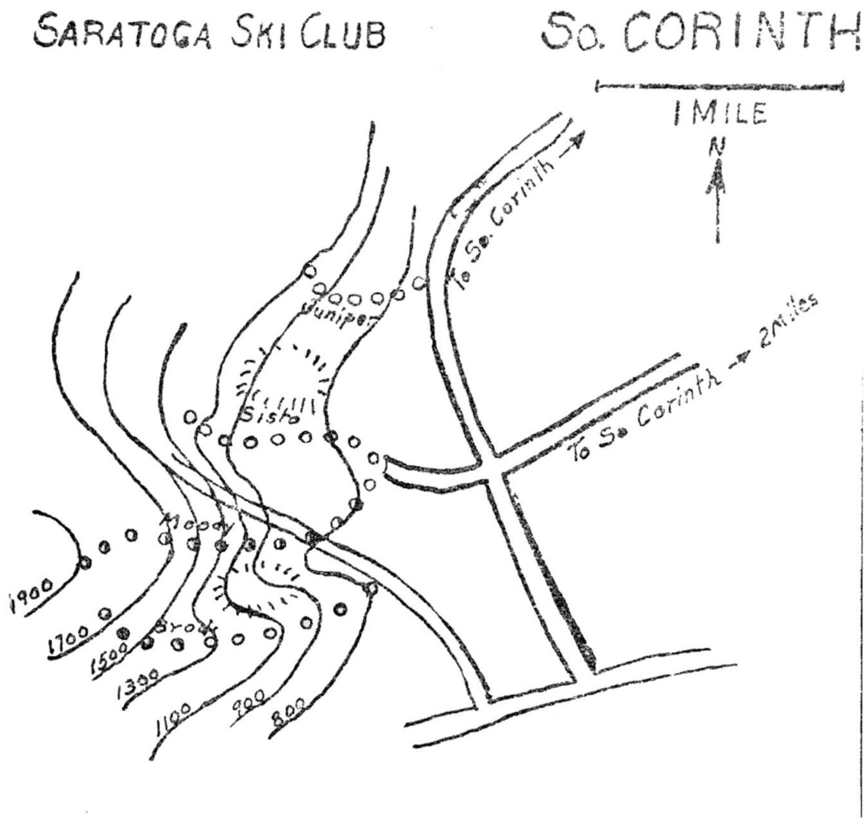

Sisto's, operated by the Saratoga Ski Club, was the precursor to Alpine Meadows. Located at Sisto's Farm, the ski area featured the Sisto Slope, which featured a rope tow. Other trails like Moody and Juniper required skiers to hike up in order to ski down. *Courtesy of the New England Ski Museum.*

Saratoga Springs, became the president of the Saratoga Ski Club and often promoted the club and its trails throughout the region.

Unfortunately, a property dispute ended the skiing at Sisto's. Toward the end of the 1937–38 winter, the owners of the property wanted to charge club members a fee to use the slopes. Members balked, and as a result, the owners strung barbed wire fencing across the trails. As a result, skiing came to end at Sisto's until 1944, when a new development called Alpine Meadows was started on the property, this time having worked out leases. It is believed that after the end of 1938, Ed Taylor relocated to Darrow's Slope in Greenfield, which was closer to Saratoga

Visiting the Area
Sisto's became Alpine Meadows in the 1940s. This area is on private property and cannot be visited. Please see the section on Alpine Meadows for more details.

ALPINE MEADOWS/ADIRONDACK SKI CENTER AND BACK TO ALPINE MEADOWS

South Corinth, New York

1944–64, 1965–86, 1987–91

Alpine Meadows Ski Area in South Corinth was the largest ski area to permanently close across all the Southern Adirondacks. Featuring nearly twenty trails and a one-thousand-foot vertical drop, it offered mainly intermediate- and beginner-level terrain, with a few expert pitches thrown in. Property disputes would plague the area throughout its existence, eventually leading to its closing, similar to its predecessor, Sisto's.

Amazingly enough, even with World War II still occurring, Ed Taylor Jr. was able to open a ski area for the 1944–45 season. Called Alpine Meadows, it was located on the former site of Sisto's, which he had operated a half decade prior. For the first season, two rope tows were built, along with a warming hut and several trails. Alpine Meadows opened on December 30, 1944, and had a very successful first ski season. For the second season of 1945–46, Taylor went to Mount Rainier to assist convalescing soldiers from World War II and used skiing as a form of physical therapy. Alpine Meadows was left in the hands of friends during that season, but he returned for 1946–47.

Taylor continued to improve his ski area throughout the rest of the 1940s and into the early 1950s. A restaurant and lodge were built on a knoll above the beginner section, and skiers would have to ride a rope tow just to make it to the lodge. Additional rope tows sprouted up across the slopes; at one point, nine rope tows were in operation. There were hardly any other ski areas in New York State or the Northeast with as many ski lifts.

The ski school was headed by Taylor himself, who also continued to operate his Alpine Sport Shop in Saratoga, named after the ski area. Teaching the

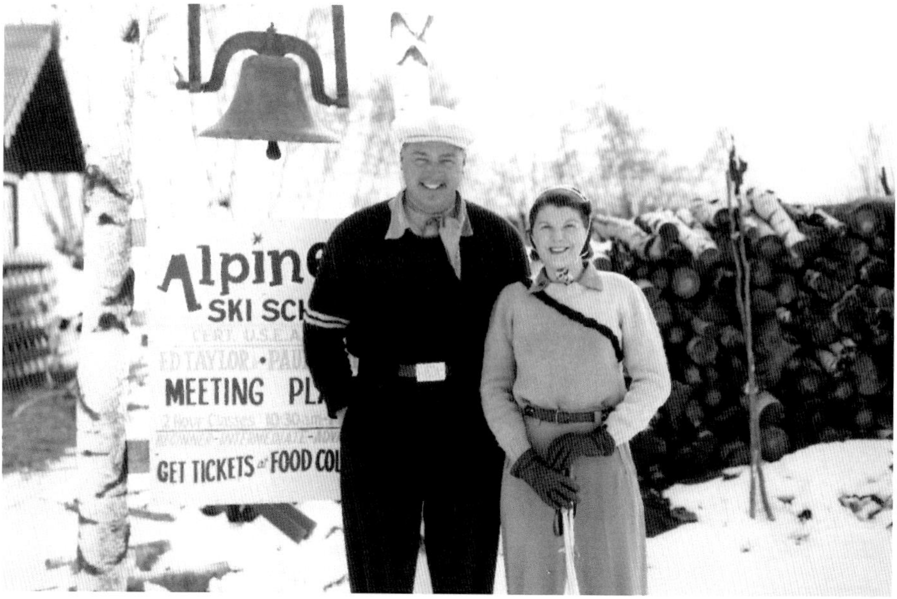

Ed Taylor Jr., pictured here with his wife, Jo, was the founder and owner of Alpine Meadows from 1946 to 1964. Pictured here in front of the ski school bell, Taylor was an expert ski instructor and taught two-hour lessons to skiers of all ability levels. *Courtesy of Linda Jo (Taylor) Stevens.*

Arlberg technique, the ski school was an affordable way to learn the sport. Linda Jo Taylor (now Stevens), Ed's daughter, remembers that many kids learned to ski for free. Her father would instruct them and then would ask them to chip in somewhere on the mountain for a fair trade. Jack Murphy, who later went to found Sugarbush Ski Area in Vermont, assisted Taylor at the ski school.

During this period, Alpine Meadows boasted "New York State's Largest Open Slope" and was well known for its wide-open skiing. Other trails, such as Powder River, provided options from the highest tow. The tows were gradually replaced with Platterpull lifts, the precursors to Pomalifts, and later a J-bar by the early 1960s. The J-bar replaced the tow that accessed the lodge. Another Platterpull would then take you from the lodge to mid-mountain, and a final Platterpull would take you to the summit.

One of the biggest promoters of the ski area was columnist Lloyd Lambert of the *Schenectady Gazette*. He glowingly spoke of Alpine Meadows and Ed Taylor, who became a personal friend. Often, Lambert would dedicate entire columns to Alpine Meadows and how much he enjoyed the ski area.

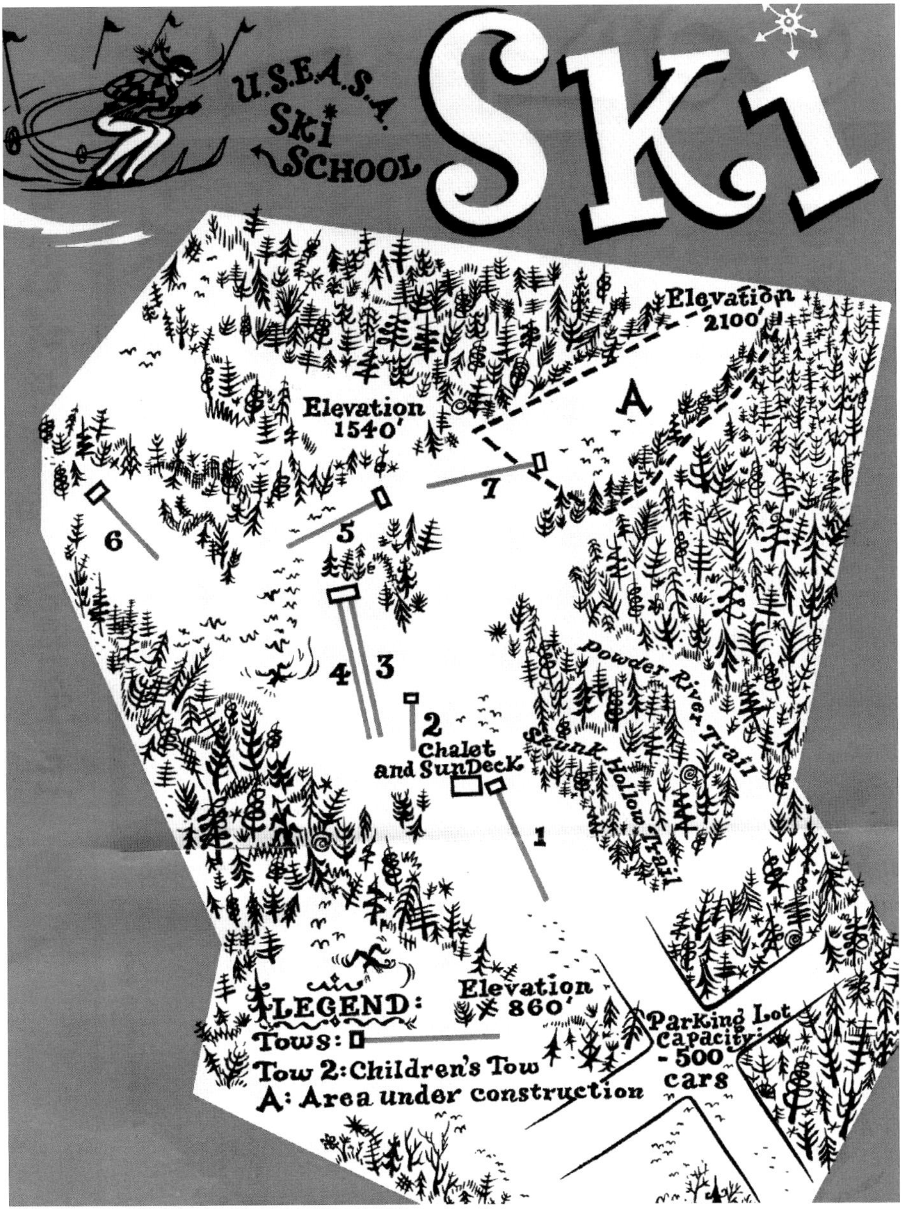

A circa late 1940s trail map of Alpine Meadows indicates a plethora of rope tows, seven at that time. Two more tows would eventually be added before some were replaced with Platterpull lifts a few years later. With a maximum of nine rope tows, Alpine Meadows has the record for most operational lifts at any lost ski area in the Adirondacks. At this time, the upper mountain was still under construction, and parking was also available for five hundred cars. *Courtesy of Linda Jo (Taylor) Stevens.*

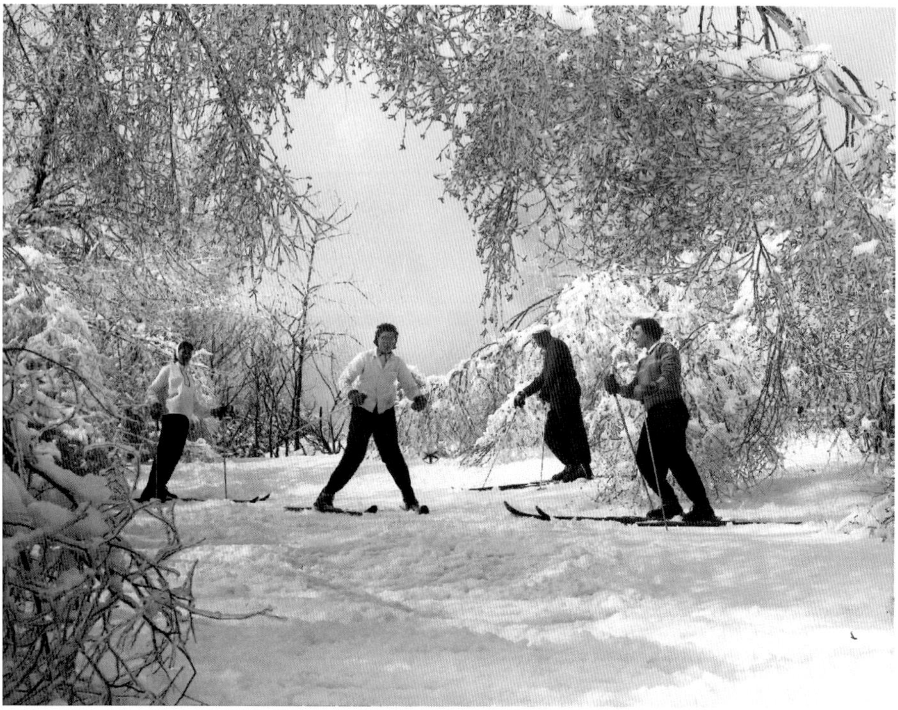

Among snow-draped trees, Ed Taylor Jr. (second from the right) teaches a class of young women a basic snowplow on a trail at Alpine Meadows. Taylor's friendly disposition put many new skiers at ease. *Courtesy of Linda Jo (Taylor) Stevens.*

Ed Taylor was one of the hardest-working ski area operators in the country. In addition to owning the ski area, he maintained the lifts, plowed the parking lots and groomed the trails on his sno-cat. He also was a salesman for Tucker Sno-Cats and the Dartmouth Ski Company and ran the Alpine Sport Shop in Saratoga Springs. His ability to run all these operations at the same time was nothing short of miraculous.

Linda Jo (Taylor) Stevens has vivid memories from growing up on the mountain at this time:

> *We used to get quite a few ski tours from New York City—one being Herman Vogel and his Skibird Tours—and one time an owl got into the eating house at night. We had a mirror which had a deer head on the top, then the mirror and the hoofs turned up to hold coats. A very heavily made up gal from the city came in looking more like she was going to the opera*

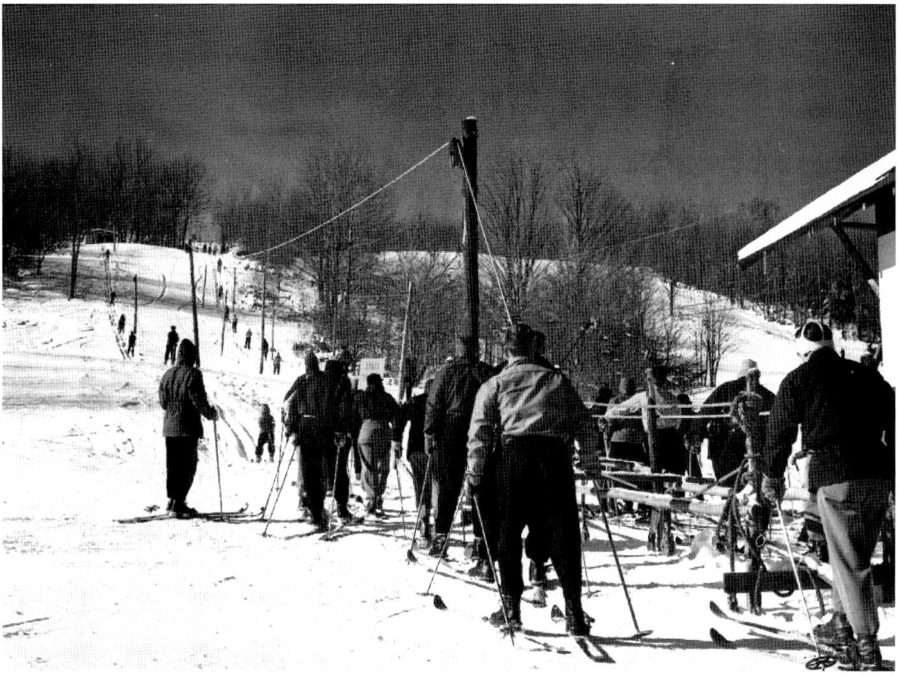

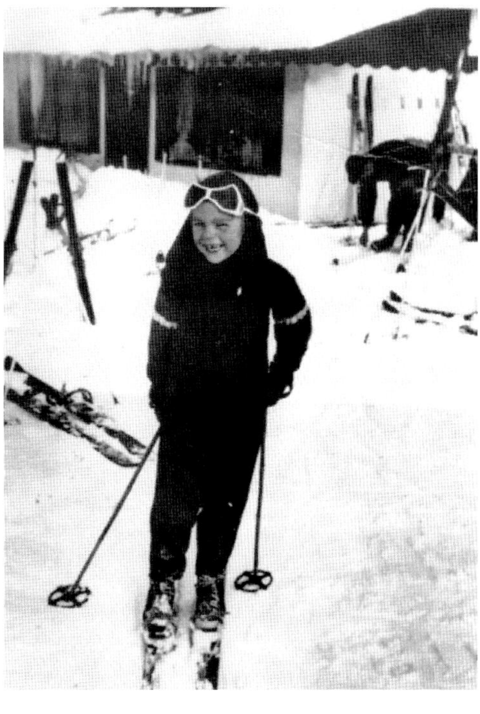

Above: A multitude of ski lifts were operational at Alpine Meadows during the first few decades of operation. Pictured here are a mid-mountain Platterpull lift on the right and a rope tow on the left, circa early 1950s. Skiers would have reached this spot by riding another Platterpull. Other rope tows were scattered around the mountain. The wide slope on the right was called Mid-Mountain Face. *Courtesy of Linda Jo (Taylor) Stevens.*

Right: Linda Jo (Taylor) Stevens, the daughter of Ed and Jo Taylor, poses for a postcard for Alpine Meadows. The lodge, seen behind her, was not located at the base of the ski area but rather on a plateau about one hundred vertical feet above the base. The lodge was accessed by a rope tow and Platterpull and featured an expansive sundeck. *Courtesy of Linda Jo (Taylor) Stevens.*

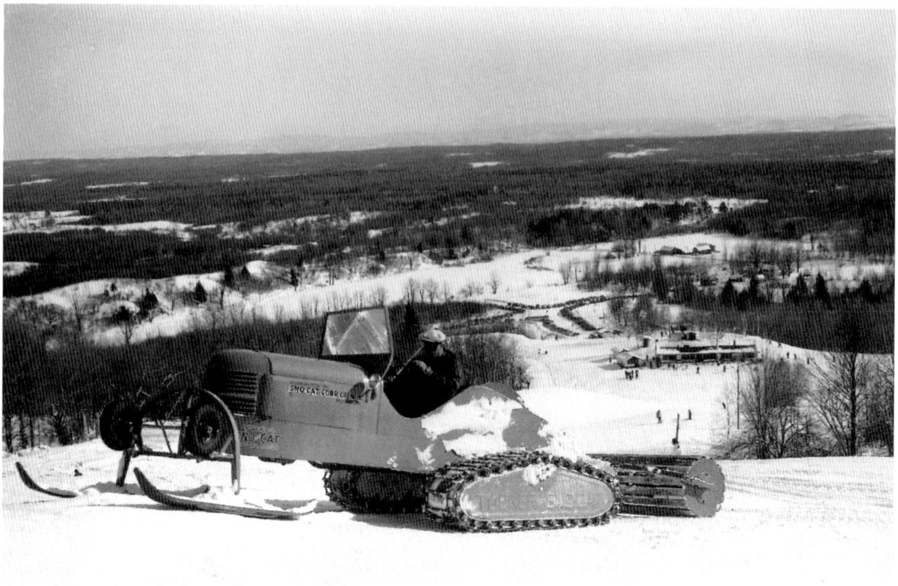

Ed Taylor Jr. is pictured here driving a Tucker Sno-Cat, grooming the snow at Alpine Meadows. The Sno-Cat was towing a wooden roller, which assisted in packing the snow. Taylor was a former representative for Tucker Sno-Cats and was quite adept at using one. A nearly full parking lot can be seen behind the lodge, as many skiers were enjoying this beautiful day. *Courtesy of Linda Jo (Taylor) Stevens.*

> *than skiing. She was putting on more mascara in the mirror, and the owl was perched on the antlers. It made a movement or noise, and she ran screaming outside. All the locals had a good laugh!*
>
> *I have lots of memories of staying overnight with girlfriends in the ski patrol hut (a real treat at the time), hearing the wolves howl on the mountain and sometimes packing with the sno-cat with my dad in the middle of the night and seeing them up by the Flatrock section.*
>
> *I also remember the guys who manned the rope tows and lifts when they rode their snow shovels down the mountain. It was always shaded and icy by 4:30 or so, and they would fly down. Every one had a heavy-duty shovel to shovel in the tow and lift lines—no snow machines in those days!*

After two decades of ownership of Alpine Meadows, Ed Taylor decided to retire. He continued to work as a salesman for the Dartmouth Ski Company, as well as the Alpine Sport Shop in Saratoga Springs. At the end of the 1963–64 season, Taylor sold off much of the infrastructure on the

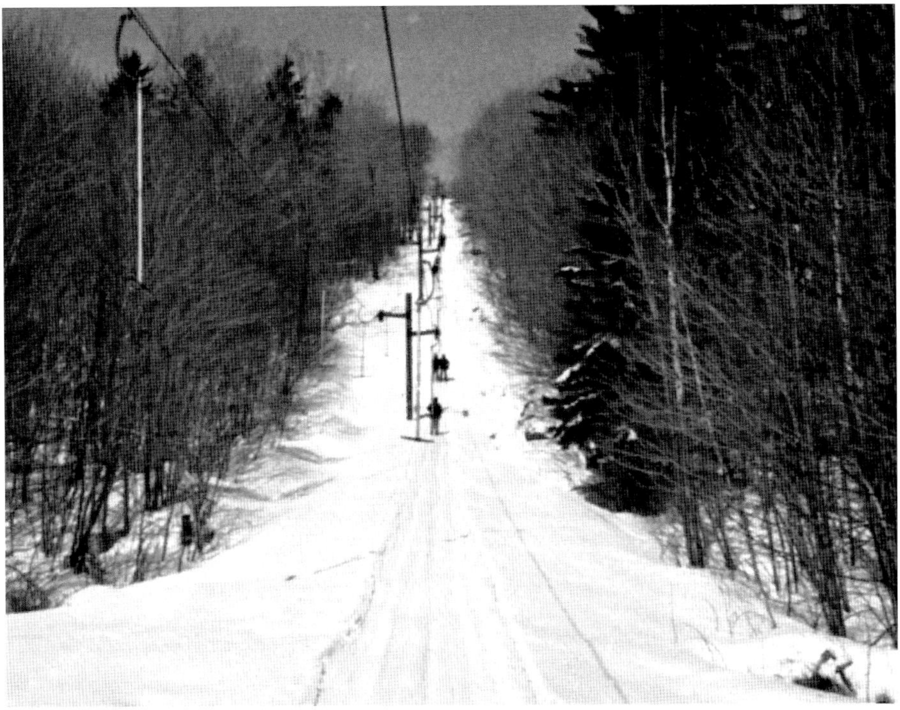

The upper-level T-bar at Adirondack Ski Center, later renamed back to Alpine Meadows, was constructed in 1968 along the former lift line of the upper Platterpull lift. The 2,500-foot-long T-bar was the ski area's longest lift and accessed a wide variety of narrower trails, as well as a slope with scattered tree islands. *Courtesy of Ron and Arlene Strader.*

mountain, including sno-cats, lifts and buildings. He planned to sell some of the lifts to "areas up north," but it is unknown if any were reinstalled elsewhere. One lift almost made it to Blister Hill in Warrensburg but, due to extensive delays, never made it there. Taylor also sold the Alpine Sport Shop to Thurlow and Dot Woodcock.

Dr. Ernest Winslow, a dentist from Corinth, had always wanted to buy a ski area. Hearing that it was for sale, he purchased the operation and reopened it for the 1965–66 ski season. He invested heavily in the ski area, building two new Hall T-bar lifts, a short beginner one and a middle T-bar that took skiers to the Flat Rock section. This was necessary, as all the other lifts had been removed. A brand-new base lodge was constructed next to the parking lot, and trails were graded and smoothed. Seeing as this was a new operation, Winslow changed the name of Alpine Meadows to the Adirondack Ski Center, highlighting its location close to the mountains.

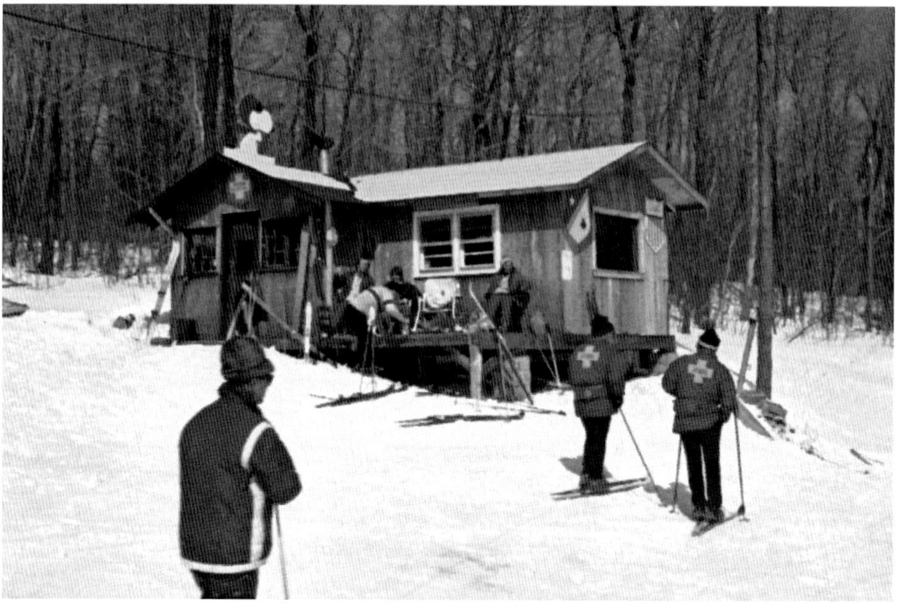

The summit rest area and ski patrol building was located at the end of the upper T-bar. A cutout of Snoopy as the Red Baron adorned the roof. The ski patrol at Alpine Meadows took pride in assisting injured skiers. Sadly, this building was lost due to arson in the early 2000s. *Courtesy of Ron and Arlene Strader.*

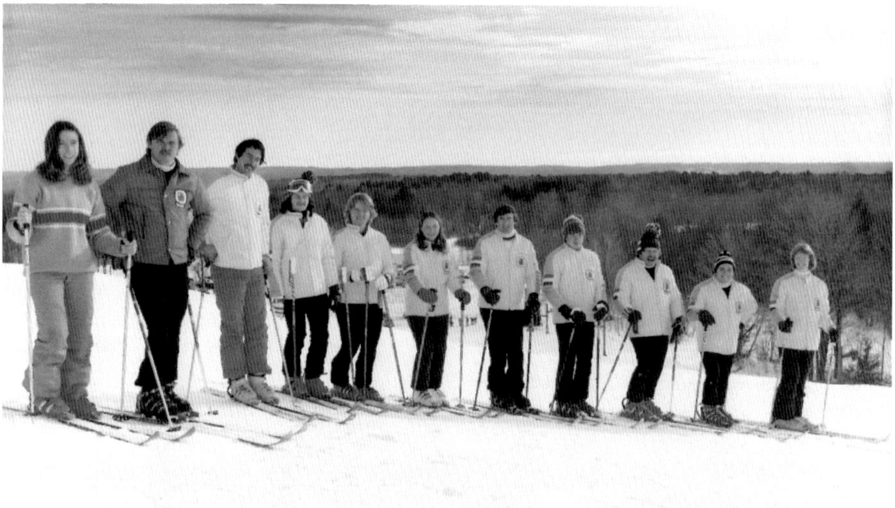

Bill Bennett (second from the left) was the ski school director at Alpine Meadows for much of the time from the late 1970s through the early 1990s. Pictured here with his fellow instructors, Bennett continued the legacy of excellent ski instructor started by Ed Taylor Jr. *Courtesy of Bill Bennett.*

Winslow continued to invest in the mountain. For the 1968–69 ski season, one of the longest T-bars in the East, at 2,600 feet, was built on the old Platterpull lift line to the summit. Once again, nearly 1,000 feet of vertical was available for skiers to enjoy. Plans were also drawn up early in his ownership for a double chair to the summit, but this would never come to fruition because of property disputes. Winslow would also purchase Royal Mountain in Caroga Lake and Moon Valley (now Titus) in Malone in the late 1960s and early 1970s. Owning these three areas at the same time must have been quite a challenge.

Alpine Meadows was a convenient place for high school and college races. Arlene Strader, whose husband, Ron, operated Darrow's, was the coach of the Saratoga High School racing team from 1966 to 1969. She would bring the students to Alpine Meadows to practice. In addition, the ski area was used on a rotating basis for races with other nearby mountains, including Royal, West Mountain and Willard.

Throughout the 1970s, Adirondack Ski Center remained a popular spot. Dave Woodcock remembers that in the early 1970s, ski instructors and patrol from the ski center would teach skiing at the Skidmore College Ski Area. Night skiing was added as well in the 1970s, and in 1977, Bill Bennett took over the ski school. He had previously worked at Brodie Mountain in Massachusetts, and at Adirondack, he made significant improvements to the school.

In the late 1970s, alternatives to traditional skiing were attempted at ski areas throughout the country. One fad was grass skiing, using rollers on the bottom of short skis. Bennett remembers that at one time in 1978, the Italian National Grass Skiing Team made a visit to Adirondack Ski Center for a demonstration. The fad never really caught on, and grass skiing ended.

New owners would take over the Adirondack Ski Center for the 1982–83 ski season. A business partnership of Tom and Jody Roohan, along with Stanton and Barbara Lawrence, purchased the ski area and renamed it Alpine Meadows. The lower and upper parcels of the ski area became under their control, with Anna Badik continuing to own the middle portion. They spruced up the base lodge and lighting system and continued to operate the ski area as a family-oriented, affordable ski area. During this time (and through the end of operations), Stewart's Ice Cream sponsored ski lessons and events for children, helping to make learning to ski affordable for as many as possible.

The Roohans and Lawrences operated the area for four seasons, until 1986. An effort was made to purchase the middle parcel of the ski area

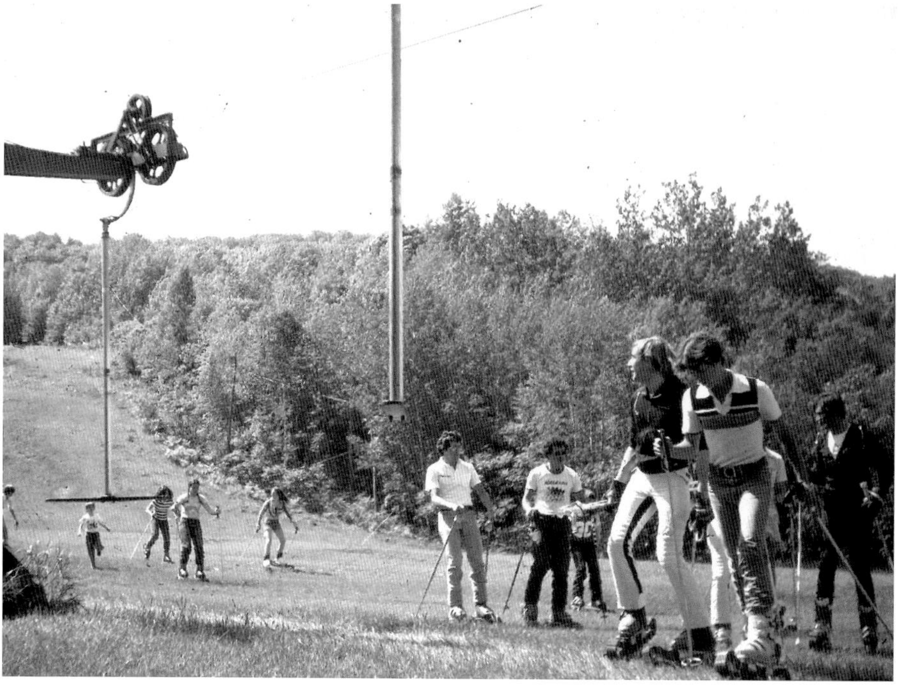

In the late 1970s, new fads began to develop at ski areas, including grass skiing. The Italian National Grass Skiing Team paid a visit to Alpine Meadows in 1978 and performed demonstrations of the sport. Alpine Meadows offered grass skiing for a short time that late summer and fall, but the sport never caught on. The grass skiing program mostly utilized the lower T-bar lift, as shown here. Just below and to the right of the middle T-bar is Jack Hay, owner of the Alpine Sport Shop in Saratoga Springs, which was once owned by Ed Taylor and owes its namesake to Alpine Meadows. *Courtesy of Bill Bennett.*

from Badik, but this was not successful. This middle parcel was needed in order to work on future expansions, such as snow making or a base-to-summit lift. Due to this property dispute, Alpine Meadows closed for the 1986–87 season.

Another valiant effort was launched in 1987 to try to open the ski area once again. This time, a lease agreement was reached with Badik, and a nonprofit organization was founded to operate the ski area. The board included Joseph Dalton of the Saratoga Chamber of Commerce; his wife, Gloria; Jack and Cathy Hay, who now owned the Alpine Sport Shop; William Healy; Ken Green; Mark Baker; Peter Sipperly; and even Ed Taylor Jr., who returned after a long hiatus from the mountain. Bill Bennett was brought in again to run the ski school, and the ski area reopened on December 27,

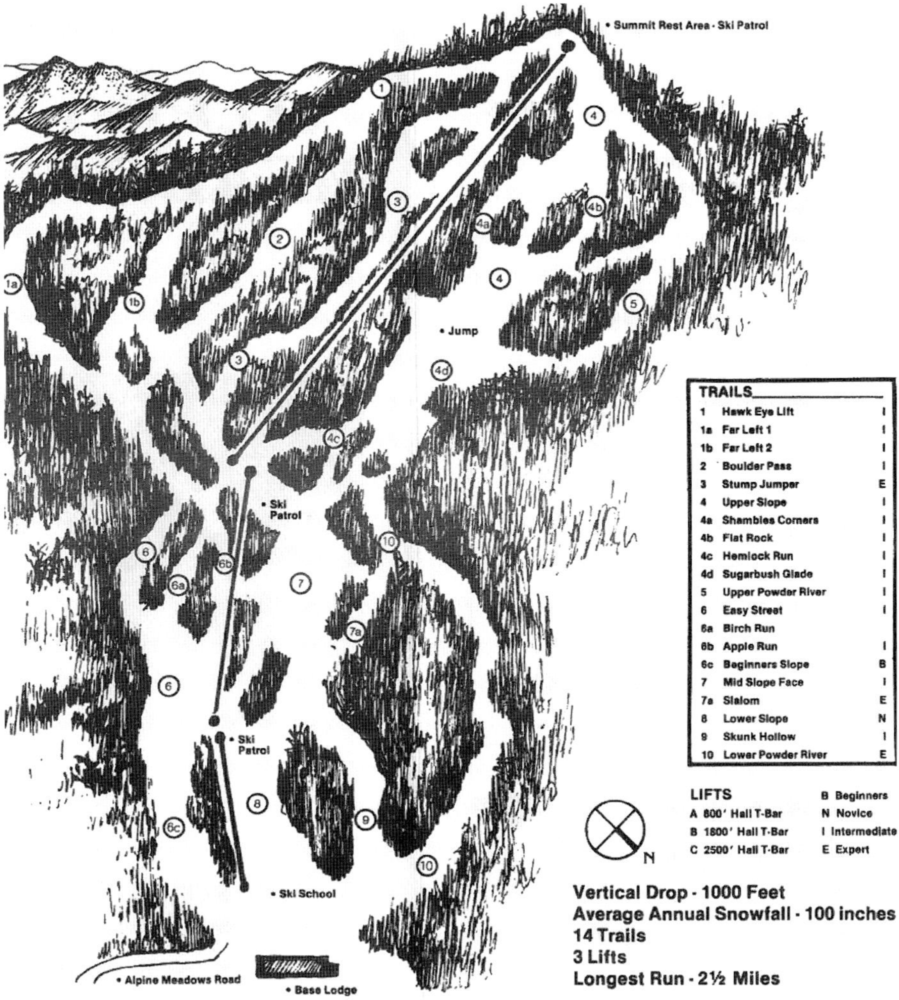

Alpine Meadows was clearly the largest ski area to be permanently lost in the Southern Adirondacks. With a vertical drop of nearly one thousand feet, three successive T-bars and twenty trails (including shorter trail sections), the mountain provided much variety. Laps could be made on one T-bar, or all three could be ridden to the summit, a process that took about twenty minutes. This 1983–84 trail map shows the final layout of the mountain.

1987. This group later dissolved, and another nonprofit group took over for the final two years of operation. For the final years of operation, Richard Rowland and his wife, Joan, managed the area. Additional committee members at that time included Jack and Helen Atwell, Leo Scheone, Eric and Teri Lis, Dave Woodcock, Mike Worth, Nick and Sue Wascho, Mark Hays and Tom Roohan.

A final property dispute led to the end of skiing at Alpine Meadows for good. Plans were drawn up for major improvements, including snow making, but without the middle parcel under ownership, they could not proceed. The area folded in 1991, never to open again. Saratoga County thus lost its last open ski area, a family ski area that had operated for nearly fifty years.

When Alpine Meadows closed, much of the equipment was left in place. Many of Alpine Meadows' trails have become overgrown with trees, though the lower portion has been kept clear, per satellite imagery. The base lodge is a private home, and the entire mountain is on private property and cannot be visited. Although Alpine Meadows is gone, the Alpine Sport Shop (www.alpinesportshop.com), owned by Jack and Cathy Hay, continues to operate and serve winter sports enthusiasts from around the region.

Visiting the Area

The ski area, located at the end of Alpine Meadows Road, is completely on private property, and visiting the area is not permitted.

PINE WOODS SKI SLOPE

Batchellerville, New York

1950–53

Today, Great Sacandaga Lake is well known as a summer vacation spot. Tourists and residents alike enjoy the lake's beaches, boating and fishing opportunities and beautiful scenery. Sixty years ago, however, a small ski area on the eastern shore attempted to bring skiers to the shores during the winter months, focusing on residents of nearby Amsterdam and Johnstown.

Pine Woods Ski Slope was founded by owner Robert W. Clark, who owned a home adjacent to the ski area, located on South Shore Road about three miles north of Batchellerville. In June 1950, he began to clear the slopes and trails on his property, installing a 1,000-foot-long rope tow. Two slopes (Novice and West Slope) and two trails were constructed, including the easier East Trail and a 1,600-foot-long narrow and winding trail for experts called the West Trail. Like many rope tow ski areas, the vertical drop was modest, topping off at only 150 feet.

The ski area was tested and pronounced fit for skiing during the weekend of December 16–17, 1950, and then opened a week later on December 23, just before Christmas. Conditions were decent for the first weekend, with fair to good skiing reported on a six-inch base. The news spread about the good skiing at Pine Woods during Christmas week, and three inches of snow on New Year's Eve improved the conditions into the beginning of 1951.

Facilities at Pine Woods were modest, with a warming hut serving refreshments and snacks. It is unknown if ski instruction was available.

Although the first ski season of 1950–51 was an initial success, subsequent years would be less successful, and the area ceased to be listed in any guidebooks or articles after 1953. It is surmised that the development of other nearby ski areas and the small nature of Pine Woods led to its closing.

Visiting the Area

No remnants of this ski area were found, as sixty years of forest growth have removed just about all traces.

Northville Winter Sports Club, the Pinnacle

Northville, New York

1936–39

The Northville Winter Sports Club was founded in Northville in the mid-1930s to promote winter activities in the village. It planned to have plenty of ice skating, skiing, tobogganing and ski jumping available to members and visitors alike.

In the fall of 1936, plans were made to open a ski center called the Pinnacle at the northern end of Hunter Creek Pond, on the east side of the village. The sports club secured a lease and worked rapidly to clear trails and slopes. A six-hundred-foot-long rope tow was installed, along with colored lights for night skiing. It was hoped that all of the work would be well received by skiers from around the region, and indeed, the area became quite popular over the next few years.

After operating for the 1936–37 ski season, improvements were made for the following year. The rope tow was replaced with an electric engine and was relocated to a different location on the same slope for easier use. It was described as being for "tired" members who enjoyed the downhill slide but disliked the long climb back up. A novice slope was built next to the tow, and the hill was graded and smoothed in December 1937. Two steeper slopes for experts were added as well. The location just a five-minute walk away from the village boosted its popularity. Additional trails on nearby hills, laid out with the assistance of Robert St. Louis of the State Conservation Department, allowed adventurous skiers to enjoy a variety of trails in the surrounding hills.

In order to ski at the area, members and guests had to purchase buttons from the Northville Winter Sports Club. These were the precursors to modern-day ski tickets.

The new tow opened in the middle of January 1938, when a large snowfall atop a firm base provided ideal conditions. First aid stations were installed, and a ski patrol provided medical assistance when needed.

Skiing would continue at the Pinnacle through the winter of 1938–39, and then the tow was moved to the George Smith Farm, north of town. It was moved to a location that had better protection from the sun and would offer the greatest variety of skiing.

Visiting the Area

Located at the north end of Hunter Creek Pond, the general location of the tow has returned to forest, and there are no remnants.

Smith Farm

Northville, New York

1940–41

The George Smith Farm, located a few miles north of the village of Northville, was the final location for the Northville Winter Sports Club's tow. It was moved in late 1939 and began operation in January 1940.

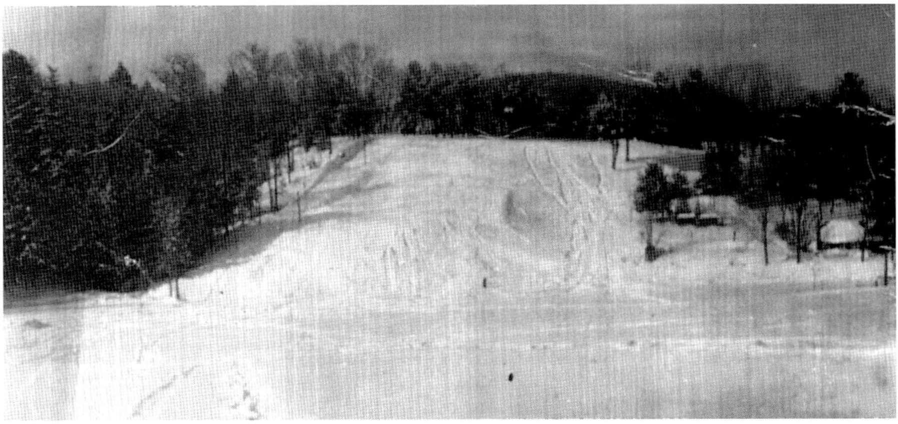

The Smith Farm Slope in Northville offered a wide-open slope with a rope tow on the left as you face the hill. Scattered trees on the right provided additional interest. Note the fresh tracks made by skiers in the deep snow. This area has been developed into homes. It has partially returned to forest and is nearly unrecognizable. *Courtesy of Gail Cramer and the Town of Northampton Archives.*

Charlie Hollearn and William Smith directed the relocation of the tow. The electrically driven lift now served an open slope, with a few scattered trees and consistent pitch throughout.

During the two winter seasons of operation at the farm, the tow was the frequent location of various school ski clubs and meets and was often used for racing. Members and townspeople continued to enjoy the tow throughout this time as well.

With the outbreak of World War II in 1941, the tow shut down and never reopened.

Visiting the Area

The tow was located near what is now the junction of Smith Beach Road and Old State Road, north of Northville. Significant housing development has removed virtually all traces of the ski area.

Pine Ridge Ski Center

Salisbury Center, New York

Circa early 1950s–76

The Pine Ridge Ski Center was a unique, classic family ski area located to the northeast of Salisbury Center. Originally owned by North Hudson Forestry, Charles Hodge purchased the property in the early 1950s and built a log cabin lodge for his family. A skier, Hodge built his own rope tow for his grandchildren on the hill behind the cabin in the early 1950s. Before long, neighborhood children discovered the area, and Hodge let them enjoy the hill. The future owner of Pine Ridge, Bill Van Allen, skied the slopes in the late 1950s using old wooden skis that his father had used in the late 1930s.

In 1961, Charles Hodge saw the opportunity to make the ski area an "official" operation. Additional trails were cleared during the summer of 1961, and a heated ski hut (still standing today) was constructed as a place for skiers to grab a bite to eat and warm up between runs. A toboggan area was created for sledders. Three runs, from 800 to 1,200 feet in length, were available from the summit. Most of these runs were carved through dense pines that had been planted decades earlier by North Hudson Forestry. The 800-foot-long rope tow that had previously been used by the Hodge family and local children was used in the new operation. The vertical drop was nearly 140 feet.

December 1961 was the grand opening for Pine Ridge. Though owned by Charles Hodge, Kenneth Gressler was the manager of the area. Mr. and Mrs. Rodney Stewart, who operated Green Acres in Dolgeville, were contracted out to run the warming hut. The area was an instant hit and often had more snowfall than other resorts, as it caught both lake effect snows as well as nor'easters moving up along the East Coast. A higher base elevation of nearly 1,100 feet allowed for cooler temperatures, which preserved the snow.

Major improvements came to Pine Ridge during the 1960s. Two other rope tows were added to the ski area, and lights for night skiing were added. A unique and original J-bar, built by the North Hudson Woodcraft Company, was built to replace the summit rope tow in 1964. This lift was a major improvement to the rope tows and was one of a kind; by the 1960s, almost all overhead cable lifts were built by major lift companies. Another J-bar was added for the 1968–69 season, replacing the beginner rope tow

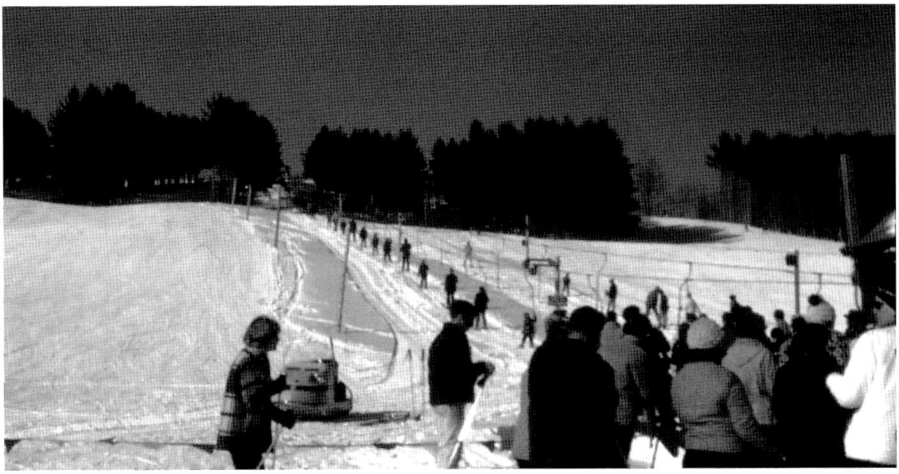

Pine Ridge featured unique dual J-bars that were manufactured by the North Hudson Woodcraft Company. The T-bar on the left went to the top, while the one on the right was for beginners and only went halfway. From the top, skiers had the choice of several wooded runs that emptied out to an open slope. Ample snowfalls, both from lake effect snows and nor'easters, allowed for skiing at Pine Ridge when other ski areas were closed. *Courtesy of Marjorie Near Roberts/Salisbury Historical Society.*

that paralleled the summit lift. The parallel J-bars was a unique feature to the ski area; no other area in the Adirondacks had this, nor did almost any ski area in the country.

By 1969, Pine Ridge featured six pine-lined trails from the top that opened to two wide-open slopes toward the bottom. Cross-country ski trails were located across the street, as was ice skating.

In 1970, Bill Van Allen, who used to ski at Pine Ridge and was now an operator of a nursing home in Little Falls, was looking to start a new career. Increased regulation had led to increasing difficulties at the nursing home, and attempts to get approval to build a new nursing home had failed. Pine Ridge was put up for sale, and Van Allen bought the ski area. The area opened in January 1971 under his ownership, but by March 1971, the new nursing home was suddenly approved.

For the next five years, Van Allen ran both Pine Ridge and built/opened the new nursing home in Little Falls. He remembers that the ski area rented out wooden skis and leather boots during this time and that the skis were built at the Adirondack Bat Factory in Dolgeville. Later improvements to the rentals included metal skis, including some that utilized the Graduated Length Method (GLM), which was a vast improvement over earlier techniques. Grooming was simple: snowmobiles dragged metal implements behind them that broke up the crust and provided a decent surface for skiing. Snow making was never installed.

The nursing home began to take up more and more of Van Allen's time, and he found he could not run the ski area at the same time. He tried to lease the ski area out, but unfortunately, that failed. In 1976, he shut down operation of the ski area for good. Portions of the J-bar were taken down, including the J-bars themselves, but some towers were left standing. The top bull wheels of each lift were left in place. Although official ski area operations ceased, family members continued to enjoy the slopes on their own, accessing the trails by hiking or by snowmobiles.

Visiting the Area

The Van Allen family continues to own and maintain the property today. Despite its having been lost as a ski area for over thirty-five years, if you stand at the base, you might even think the ski area is still in operation. The trails remain mostly clear of tree growth, portions of the J-bars are still standing and the ski hut remains as well.

Pine Ridge is found a few hundred feet east of the junction of Rice and Ukrainian Roads and is located on Ukrainian Road. The family does not discourage skiers and sledders from accessing the property, but please be very respectful and avoid the log cabin area.

Gold Mine Hill at Hibbard Farm

Salisbury Corners, New York

1942

One of the briefest rope tow ski areas to operate in the foothills of the Southern Adirondacks was at Gold Mine Hill at the Hibbard Farm. Operated by the Penguin Winter Sports Club, this facility was only open for a few months in early 1941.

The Penguin Winter Sports Club had operated a rope tow for members in nearby Dolgeville in 1941. While it was popular, a better location was sought. Fundraisers were held in late 1941 to raise money to move the tow. Ransom Hill on the Little Falls Road in Dolgeville was initially eyed, but a club member secured a better lease at Jack Hibbard's Farm in Salisbury Corners in December. Better known as Gold Mine Hill, this area was described as having one "of the sportiest slopes in the state." Club members worked rapidly to remove fencing and clear rocks from the slope. As it was late December, this must have been difficult work.

Work began on erecting the tow in January 1942. On January 4, members met at the Volks Hotel in Salisbury Corners and then moved over to Gold Mine Hill. Some poles for the rope tow were installed, along with the engine the following weekend. On the weekend of January 17–18, the rope was spliced, and final towers were erected on the slope. Some club members gave the slope a try before the lift became operational, but snow depths were quite thin and unsatisfactory.

In order to increase interest for the new development, a membership drive was held, and twenty-eight new members were added to the rolls. Finishing touches were completed on the tow in late January. Everything was in place for an official opening—except for a heavy snowfall. The cover was too thin in January to allow this. However, by early February, the situation had changed, and snow arrived.

A "soft" opening was held on Saturday, February 7, to test out the tow. There were some kinks to work out with the engine and the rope; however, those were worked out for the grand opening on Sunday. During the grand opening, more than fifty club members and local skiers enjoyed fresh, fast snow, and slalom racing was held. The club pronounced the operation a success.

Skiing continued, mainly on weekends, at Gold Mine Hill through the month of March. A fundraiser was held at the Volks Hotel on March 6, where dancing and oyster stew were enjoyed.

Outside of Salisbury Corners, the world was certainly changing. Throughout February and March, air raid drills and blackout exercises were performed. World War II was ramping up, and it can only be imagined that skiing provided a bit of an escape for nervous residents.

Plans were made by the club to attempt to reopen the tow for the 1942–43 season. But the gasoline restrictions on both the tow and skiers' cars made operation difficult or impossible. Some cross-country ski events were held by the club, but it is not believed that the tow operated that season. The tow was then abandoned, not only because of the war but also due to a "lack of new blood in the organization." Subsequently, the tow and equipment were moved to Dolgeville in 1946–47 when the Penguin Club attempted to reorganize.

Harry Foster, whose great-uncle Jack Hibbard owned the property, remembers seeing the towers on the slope while growing up. He remembers hearing that the slope would quickly melt out in the springtime, as it faced due south. This may also have factored into the decision to not reopen the tow after World War II.

Visiting the Area
Gold Mine Hill is on private property and is inaccessible. However, the slope can still be seen, reforested, approximately one-third of a mile east of Salisbury Corners. Park at the country store and look across the street at Gold Mine Hill, where you can see the overgrown slope.

INDIAN HILL

Barneveld, New York

1962–91

Indian Hill, located off Old Poland Road in Barneveld, was a classic family ski area. It was in operation for nearly thirty years, providing an affordable location for skiers of all ages to enjoy the sport. Rising insurance costs, compliance with regulations and the changing ski scene led to Indian Hill closing at the end of the 1990–91 ski season.

The Haskell family—Glen and Betty—was instrumental in the operation of this area. In 1961, they moved to a larger farm on Old Poland Road to accommodate their growing family. Behind this property was a small hill that a neighbor, Bob Collins, had shown interest in clearing for sledding. In 1962, Henry Miller and other local skiers were scouring the area to try to find a location for a ski area. They came across the Haskells' property and offered them the chance to lease it out to a new ski organization they were forming. The Haskells agreed, leasing it to them for one dollar a year. Betty Haskell had the chance to name the future ski area on their property, and she called it Indian Hill based on legend that some of the mounds on the property were Indian burial grounds.

Trails were cleared on the hill, and a rope tow was constructed and opened for the 1962–63 ski season. The Haskells' farmhouse became essentially the base lodge, where children could warm up between runs by the fire, sip some

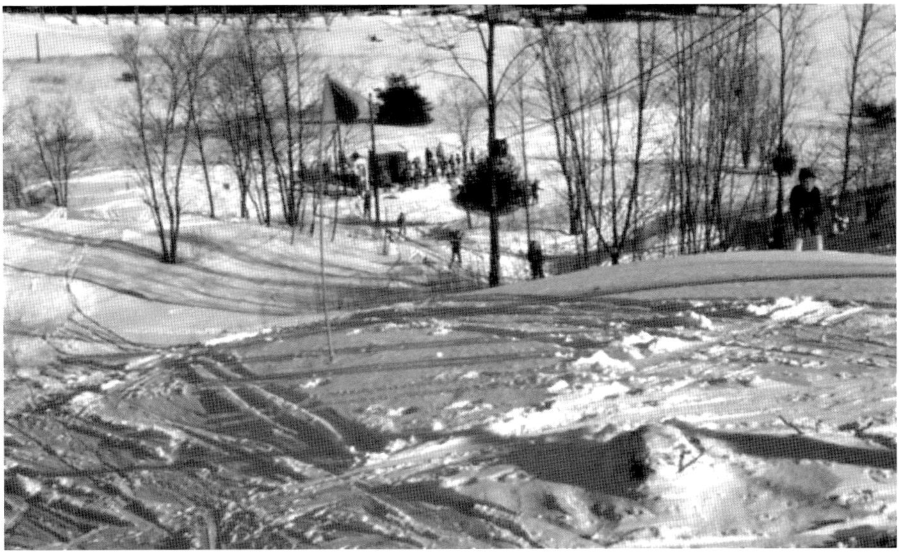

Indian Hill, a club-operated ski area in Barneveld, was a wonderful ski area for families. Here, young skiers hold tightly onto the rope tow on their ride to the top. The tow on the left would eventually be replaced by a handle tow for easier riding. Sadly, rising costs resulted in this ski area closing in 1991. *Courtesy of Bronwyn Davis.*

hot chocolate and wait for their parents to pick them up. The Haskells were extremely generous to all the families of the Indian Hill Ski Association. Their nine children—Geno, Trudy, Neal, Mary Alice, Truman, Bernard, Andrew, Bettina and Christopher—all grew up at the ski area and have many fine memories.

Throughout the 1960s and 1970s, Indian Hill grew in both membership and facilities. Night skiing was added as an amenity. Dick Villiere, a ski coach originally from Old Forge, moved to within a quarter mile of Indian Hill in 1965. He started a ski racing program at Indian Hill, where students learned the fundamentals of racing and became top-notch local and regional racers. Downhill racing events, including slalom skiing, were often held at Indian Hill for members, as it was a bit too small to hold regional events. Nordic races, including New York State Section III events and Bill Koch Races, were held on cross-country trails built throughout the property.

In the 1970s, a new warming hut was built at the immediate base of the ski area, as more space was needed for growing programs. The rope tow was also rebuilt during this time, as regulations required the engine to be placed at the bottom of the tow. For the 1981–82 ski season, the rope tow was replaced by a brand-new handle tow, providing easier access to the summit. Fundraisers were often held to help pay for the operation and improvements, including "dime-a-scoop" suppers, where members would pay ten cents for every scoop of food.

Although the new lift was a significant improvement, the changing ski industry began to take its toll at Indian Hill. Increased liability insurance proved costly, and various state regulations made the operation more difficult. In 1985, the Haskells' youngest child, Christopher, left for college. Still, the Haskells continued to lease the property to the association.

By 1990, costs had soared, and the area almost did not open for the 1990–91 season. After pleas from the members, annual fees were raised to ninety dollars per family, and enough rejoined that year to keep Indian Hill in operation for one more year. Sadly, in June 1991, Betty Haskell passed away. The board of directors tried to make plans to open the area for the 1991–92 season, but as they were making plans, Glen Haskell passed away in December. With the passing away of the owners of the property, the area had to close, and skiing at Indian Hill came to an end.

The handle tow was removed and sold to the nearby town of Remsen, where it helped to reopen the Little Alpine Ski Area for a few years. That lift is still in place and may someday be reactivated for a tubing hill. Slowly, trees and brush began to take over the slope, and today, the area is mostly reforested.

In 2007, Bronny Davis, whose family learned to ski at Indian Hill, published an excellent history of the area called *Tales of Indian Hill: The Biggest Little Ski Area*, which included many memories of members. It contains numerous photos and is a wonderful tribute to the ski area.

Indian Hill also lives on through former members and their families. For instance, Bernard Haskell is now a race director at Quechee Ski Area in Vermont and learned his lifelong passion at the ski area. He recalled:

> *I live for winter and skiing and I have been very involved in ski racing at the junior level for many years. The one thing I learned was that I want every child I work with in ski racing to become the best they can in their short racing career, but along the way teach them the skiing fundamentals that will carry them through a life of skiing. Skiing is a sport for life, and if they can share the passion of skiing with their children, a little of Indian Hill will carry on forever!*

Mary Alice (Haskell) Hallett will always remember Indian Hill:

> *I have many wonderful memories of Indian Hill. Drinking hot chocolate and eating hot dogs at the annual winter festival, skiing under the lights on cold, starry nights and bombing down from the top of the ski hill all the way down to our house, without using my poles once. My parents were very proud of the fact that Indian Hill was a safe place for kids to hang out with their friends and ski all day. I often run into people from Barneveld who will tell me that Indian Hill had a positive impact on their childhood, and to this day, they still ski with many of their old friends from Indian Hill.*

Visiting the Area
Indian Hill is on private property on Old Poland Road just south of the railroad tracks in Barneveld and is not accessible to the public.

Remsen Central School

Remsen, New York

Circa 1959–60

The Remsen Central School was the location for a brief rope tow in 1959 and 1960 and served as a "seedling" area for the future Little Alpine Ski Area in town. It was used almost exclusively by students.

Don Clemmons, who lived near the school, noticed in the late 1950s that children were using the hill in front of the school for sledding. A skier, Clemmons had made a trade of a tractor for a portable rope tow from a friend in 1959. Hearing that he had the tow, the principal, John Bishop, asked him if he could install the tow at the school. Clemmons obliged. It was used in early 1959 and again for the 1959–60 ski season. Clemmons had trouble finding assistance to operate the tow and decided to close the lift, which was later sold. Two years later, in 1962, he founded the Little Alpine Ski Area a short distance away, which operated off and on for nearly three decades.

Visiting the Area

There are no remnants of this ski area due to its brief existence, but the slope that once featured the tow can easily be seen directly in front of the Remsen Central School.

Little Alpine

Remsen, New York

1962–71, 1976–83, 1992–95

Little Alpine was a classic community ski area that operated in the town of Remsen over several decades, with several periods of inactivity between operations. Although the slope was short and the vertical small, it was the perfect area for children and beginners. It is no longer in operation, but there have been recent plans to reactivate the ski lift to be used for tubing.

About two years passed between the operation of the first tow in Remsen and the second ski area, which would be known as Little Alpine. In 1962, after running the first tow in Remsen, Don Clemmons was approached by the principal at the school, John Bishop, to consider opening another ski area for the children in town. Clemmons was convinced and began to plan for a ski area. He had initially sought permission from the Memorial Field Board to operate a ski area next to the field, but since most of its members were not skiers, they initially said no. Clemmons walked out of the meeting but heard shortly after from the board that it had a change of heart. An insurance rider for skiing was added to its policy.

Next came the clearing of the slope. Clemmons sought the help of Jerry Blood, who was active in the community, to help clear the field above the baseball diamond in Remsen. Initially full of rocks, stumps and brush, the slope was smoothed and graded to a perfect beginner/low intermediate pitch. In the fall of 1962, Clemmons and a new committee—consisting of Doug Hughes (a mechanic), Don Seubert (who owned the local lumberyard), John Bishop (the school principal) and Al Dimartino (a mechanic with Mohawk Airlines)—worked to build the tow. A Ford truck was hauled to the slope and mounted, and holes for the rope tow towers were dug. Wet weather made

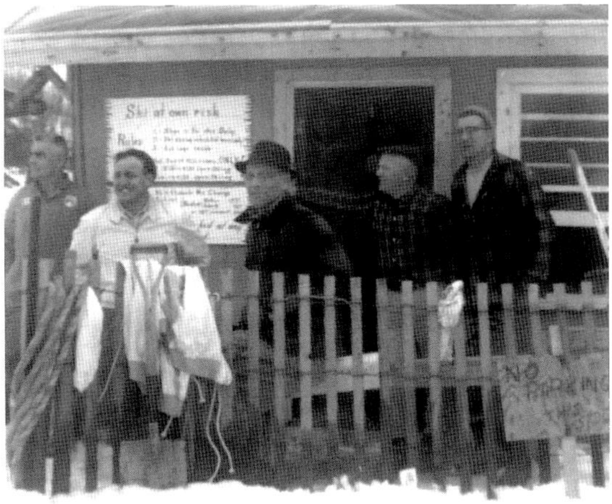

Several volunteers from Little Alpine gather at the base of the tow. *From left to right*: Doug Hughes, John Bishop, Al Dimartino, Don Clemmons and Don Seubert. Clemmons was the founder of the area and worked hard to make sure that skiing would be an option in the town of Remsen. *Courtesy of Don Clemmons.*

the hill a "bloody mess," according to Clemmons, making the lift installation difficult. A Mr. Evans, who worked at Snow Ridge, helped procure parts for the ski lift.

The ski area opened for the first time for the Christmas holiday in 1962 and was an instant hit. Schoolchildren thronged the area, and a system was set up to make sure they actually knew how to ski. A novel ticket system, consisting of a red tag for absolute beginners and green tags for approved skiers, helped to ensure that children would not get hurt. They had to earn their green tags, a source of pride. Clemmons remembers that one child named Mark worked extra hard to finally earn his green tag. While in college, this student returned and expressed his gratitude to Don for taking the time to teach him to ski, one of his proudest moments.

A name was needed for this new operation. A contest was held at the school, with the winning name "Little Alpine." In a later operation, a slogan was added—"Ski Where Dragons Sleep." Dragons are a symbol of the Welsh people and a nod to local residents, many of whom are of Welsh ancestry.

Skiing was free for children, and though out-of-town residents had to pay one or two dollars to enjoy the slope, it was still a terrific bargain. A snack bar, run by Ethel Delong, served hot dogs, hamburgers and hot chocolate. Although it took much convincing to run the snack bar, Clemmons said that Delong greatly appreciated the opportunity and really enjoyed watching the kids ski.

Donna Kagiliery, daughter of Don Clemmons, enjoyed skiing at Little Alpine. She remembers that she and other students had to climb the hill after fresh snowfalls and sidestep the hill to pack the snow.

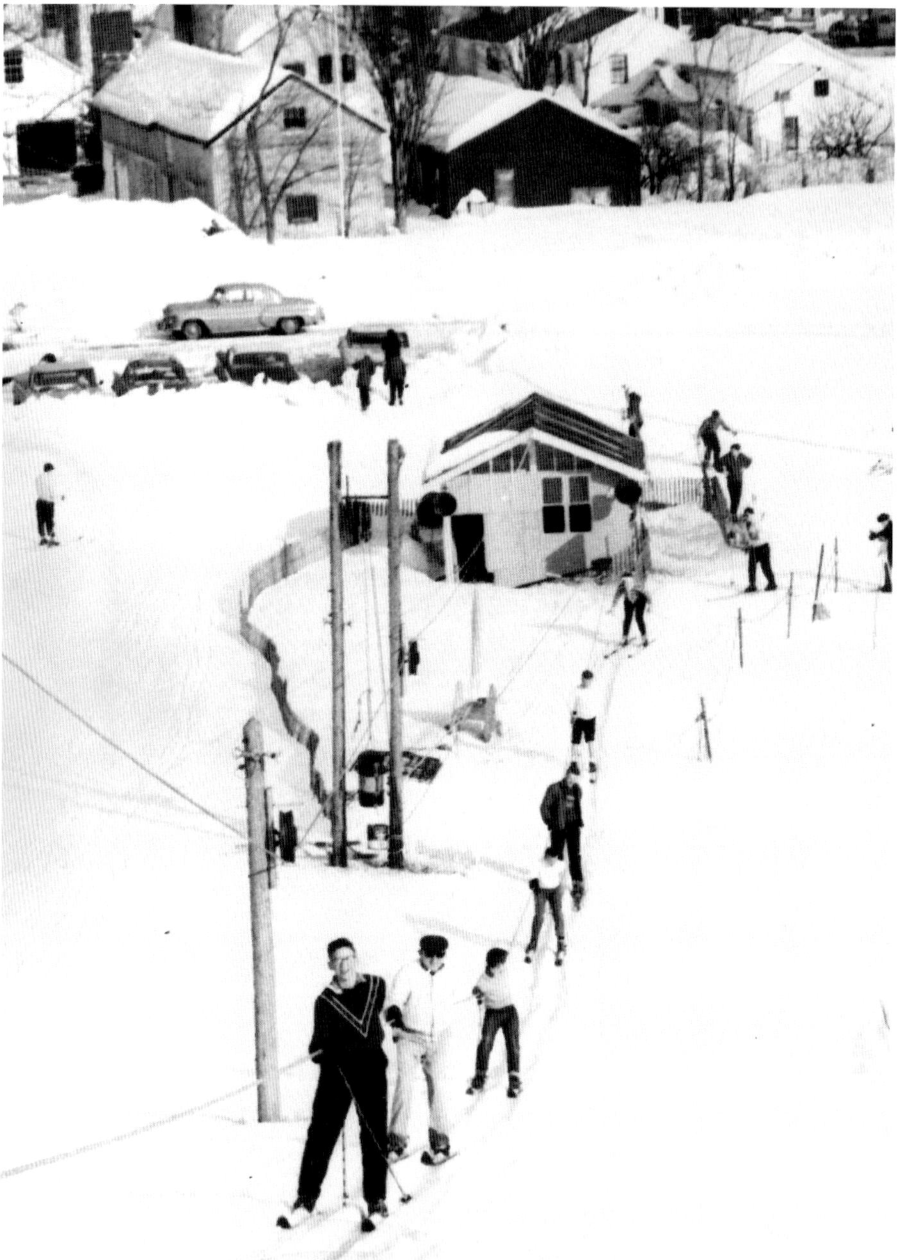

This rope tow was the first ski lift at Little Alpine and offered skiing on an eighty-foot vertical drop. Skiers would often ride the lift as a group, as this was the easiest way to enjoy the tow. Portions of this tow still stand as of 2012. *Photo by Bruce Phelps, courtesy of Don Clemmons.*

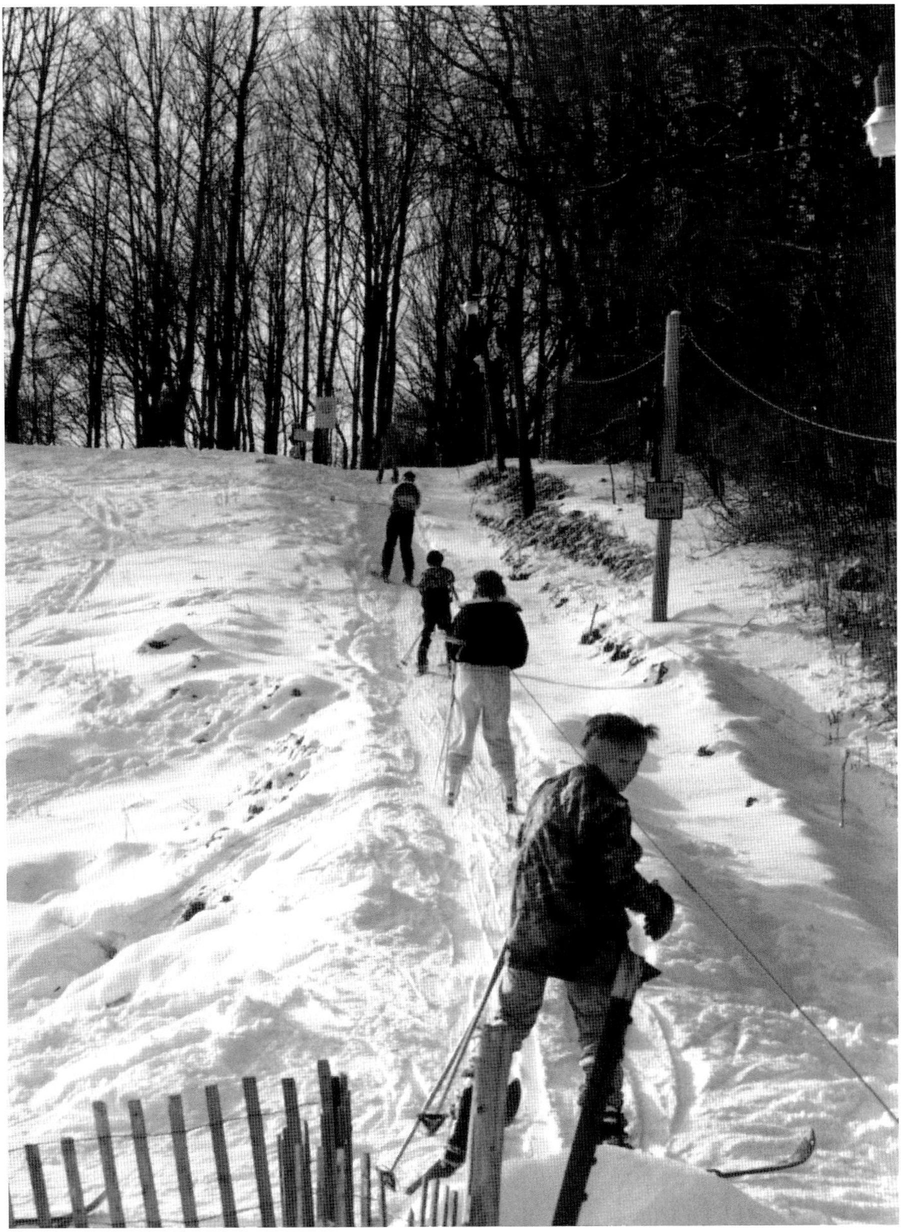

The rope tow at Little Alpine was later replaced by a more modern handle tow, as seen here in this early 1990s photo. Note the rope tow towers that were still standing and continue to stand today. The handle tow was easier to ride than the rope tow and did not cause damage to gloves, as rope tows do. *Courtesy of the Town of Remsen.*

Night skiing was also enjoyed at Little Alpine on Friday and Saturday nights. Lights from a nearby baseball field extended the hours of operation. Oftentimes, kids had to be made to leave at the end of a night skiing session, as they were having so much fun.

By 1965, Clemmons had moved on from the ski operation, as his employment at General Electric began to take up much of his time. Other volunteers continued to operate the area until about 1971, and then it fell into a period of inactivity. This was likely due to a lack of volunteers and higher energy costs during that period. In 1976, volunteers reopened the area, which proved popular once again until 1983. In that year, vandals burned down the ski lift, shutting down the operation for nearly a decade.

Undaunted, a new group of volunteers, including Peter Billard and Gregory Roos of the town's Recreation Committee, decided to reopen the area for a final time for the 1991–92 ski season. A used handle tow lift from the now defunct Indian Hill Ski Area was obtained, and it was refurbished and installed at Little Alpine. The area had a grand reopening on February 1, 1992, and once again, skiing returned to Remsen. More than fifty people contributed a combined total of hundreds of hours to help reopen the area.

This last incarnation of Little Alpine ran until 1995, when it finally closed for good, due to many factors. The handle tow was left in place and the slope was maintained, being used for sledding during winter. In the past few years, plans have been discussed to reopen the area for tubing. Bruce Phelps, who skied at Little Alpine while in high school, has been working on refurbishing the tow. Perhaps one day, lift-served winter sports will return to Little Alpine.

Visiting the Area

Little Alpine is an easily accessible location that can be explored freely. The former ski area is located off Steuben Street, just west of Main Street, with parking available just behind the post office near the athletic field. The former ski slope remains clear and maintained today, and at the time of this writing, the Pony lift is also still standing. Efforts are being made to restore the Pony lift to be used for tubing, so perhaps in the future, Little Alpine will once again serve local families as a place for downhill enjoyment.

Remnants of the former rope tow—including the lift towers—are also found just to the right of the Pony lift as you face the hill. Lights that were used for night skiing are also still mounted on the former rope tow towers.

Chapter 4

LOST SKI AREAS OF THE SPECULATOR–OLD FORGE REGION

Seven ski areas have been lost in the Speculator–Old Forge region. Most were relatively brief rope tows, but two—Maple Ridge in Old Forge and Silver Bells in Wells—were significant areas.

The snow trains in the mid-1930s and early 1940s played an important role in the development of the Maple Ridge complex in Old Forge. Hundreds of skiers from Utica and Syracuse would arrive via these trains to enjoy the open slope and rope tow at Maple Ridge. Additional trails and tows were constructed over the next ten to twenty years, and the ski area became a very popular location. The development of nearby McCauley Mountain led to Maple Ridge becoming more of a training area for students in town, and in the early 1990s, it was closed. Today, it is one of the easiest locations to explore, with lots of remnants to see.

Silver Bells in Wells was in existence for about fifteen years and was a family ski area with a T-bar and several trails. Easily accessible via Route 30 from Amsterdam, the ski area was popular on weekends. Trails were available for all ability levels. A lack of snow making and financial difficulties led to the area closing in the late 1970s.

Raquette Lake, a small hamlet in the town of Long Lake, once had three rope tow ski areas, a unique situation for an area with a low winter population. The tow was relocated three different times: once on the Antlers Golf Course, then on Brown Tract Road and finally on Mick's Hill in the center of the hamlet. Winter carnivals were enjoyed at Mick's Hill, but a lack of volunteers and high liability costs led to its closing.

SILVER BELLS

Wells, New York

1961–71, 1973–77

The Silver Bells Ski Area was a classic family ski area with modest facilities. Opening in 1961, it ran for ten years before closing for two. It would later reopen and last for four more seasons when a combination of a lack of snow making, a lack of investment capital and competition ad resulted in its closure.

Thomas and Amelia "Milly" Novosel were the founders of Silver Bells. Thomas owned the Novosel Lumber Company in Speculator, where the couple had lived since the early 1940s. In 1961, they decided to open a ski area and purchased two hundred acres of land in nearby Wells from Hiram Babcock. Bulldozers and chainsaws cleared the trails in the latter part of the summer of 1961. Four trails were cut that first year, ranging from beginner to expert on a 400-foot vertical drop. An 1,800-foot-long Hall T-bar lift was built as the only lift to the summit, with a beginner rope tow serving an easier slope. A cozy base lodge was also built, which had a full view of the trails and slopes.

Staff was hired to help run the ski area, including Don Leadley, who would manage the mountain; Dick Lambert, who would run the ski school; Amos Page; who would assist Lambert; and Jack Leadley, who would direct the ski patrol. The ski area opened on December 16, 1961, with a day of free skiing and events. Santa Claus paid a visit, along with a costumed character "Magoo," who was known for his antics on the slopes. In January 1962, Hiram Babcock, who had sold the land for the ski area, took his first lesson. At seventy-seven years old, he had never tried the sport before but had a terrific time.

The rest of the first year of skiing went well, and over the next few years, another trail was added and existing trails were improved. In 1964, Lloyd Lambert, writing for the *Schenectady Gazette*, described the trails:

> *Advancing from the rope tow area to the T-bar, the person capable of controlled skiing has a choice of several trails. The Logger wanders back to the base in easy stages; the Sawdust trail, the one that is most popular, has a rather steep section at the top of the trail graduating to an easy run to the base. This latter trail gets its name from the fact that the entire trail was covered with sawdust at the time of construction to cover any rough ground.*

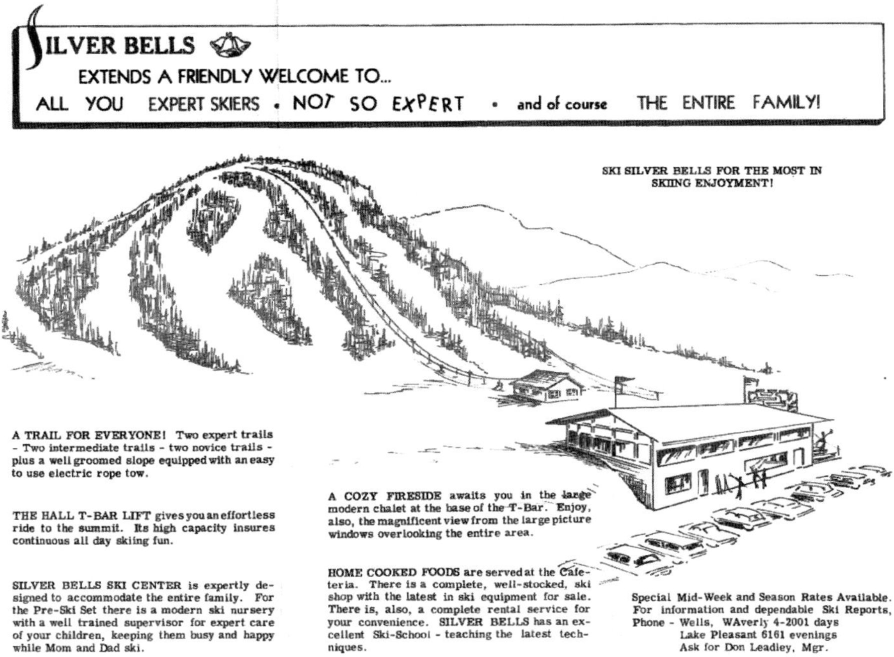

Silver Bells, located in Wells, was a classic family ski area. One of the larger lost areas, it had a Hall T-bar and rope tow and seven trails on a four-hundred-foot vertical drop. This brochure interior shows a map of the ski area, along with a description of the facilities, including a modern ski school and lodge with a cozy fireplace and home-cooked foods. *Courtesy of Jon Regan.*

> *Those who like a little more challenge can select the Hemlock. This trail is classed as intermediate, dropping away from the top at a pretty good pitch with moguls to add interest. The well-advanced skier may wish to try the Whip; this trail can really whip you into shape if you think you are good.*

Many people learned to ski for the first time at Silver Bells. Peter Cohen was one of them and describes his first day:

> *Silver Bells was the first area I ever skied. I only went there once but I remember it well. It was December 1965, and I was nine. I was relegated to the small rope tow at beginner's hill (my older sisters and dad made it up the T-bar, their first day of skiing also), and I had great difficulty using the tow. It was only at the end of the day that I made it to the top of the slope with my dad's assistance. I remember that first run where I schussed*

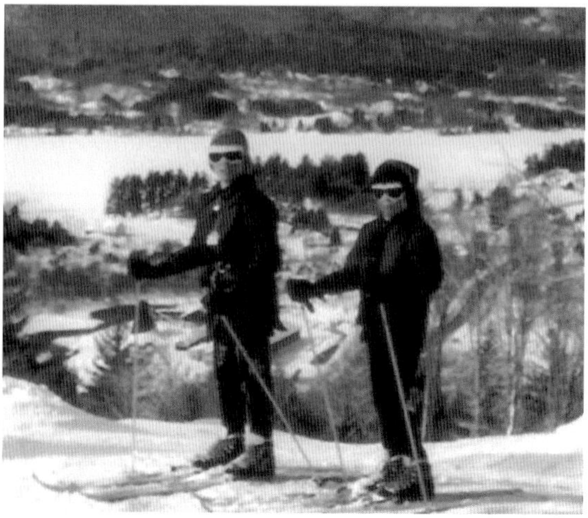

Frequent skiers to Silver Bells, Gary and Park Pavlus pose at the start of the expert Whip Trail. The Whip was frequently the location of slalom racing events. The town of Wells and Lake Algonquin can be seen in the background. *Courtesy of Mark Pavlus.*

> *straight down the hill and plowed into the crowd at the bottom. I was mighty proud.*

A few years later in 1968, the Novosels purchased Oak Mountain in Speculator, and special joint tickets were offered with Silver Bells. Special events continued at Silver Bells during this time, including an annual "Snow Queen" contest. Snowmobile races were also popular at the ski area.

In December 1971, a period of warm weather plagued the Northeast, and without snow making, Silver Bells didn't open. When the snows finally did arrive, it was too late. The Novosels concentrated their attention at Oak Mountain, and Silver Bells didn't operate for the 1972–73 winter either.

Timberline Homes, a home construction company, purchased the defunct ski area from the Novosels in 1973. The ski area was refurbished, and a pond for ice skating was dug. The company hoped to make the ski area private, with limited memberships, and run it as a club. It hoped to have as many as 120 members, which would help subsidize improvements like a chairlift to the left of the T-bar. For the 1973–74 season, the area remained open to the public and to the members of the new private club.

Like many private ski club ideas across the Northeast over the past three or four decades, success was not found. Joining a private club is an expensive endeavor and often limits a family to just that ski area. In addition, limited facilities of just a T-bar and five trails were not enough to keep sustained interest.

From 1974 to the ski area's closing in 1977, John and Linda Callahan, along with Ken Croucher, managed the ski area as a public, family area. It was only open on weekends and holidays. Finally, the area closed after the winter of 1976–77 due to increased competition, a lack of investment and no snow making. The T-bar lift was removed, perhaps installed elsewhere, and the slopes have gradually returned to forest. Recent satellite imagery suggests that portions of the former ski area have been logged.

Visiting the Area

Silver Bells is located on private property and is not able to be visited. It is, however, still visible from Route 30. At the junction of Route 30 and Buttermilk Hill Road, travel south on Route 30 for half a mile. You will then see Silver Bells on your left. If you look closely enough, you can still make out the line for the T-bar.

Scribner Slope

Speculator, New York

1937–49

Speculator is one of the snowiest villages in all of New York State, and with consistent cold temperatures, it remains a winter sports destination today. Its early ski development consisted of two rope tow areas and other open slopes. In the late 1940s, Oak Mountain took over the ski scene. The rope tow areas—Scribner Slope and Page Hill at Melody Lodge—folded once Oak opened for the 1948–49 ski season.

The Speculator Winter Sports Club developed a series of trails and slopes around the village in the mid-1930s. For the 1937–38 ski season, $50,000 in funding was received from the WPA, and an 800-foot-long tow was installed at the property of Mr. and Mrs. Russ Scribner. A slope was designed by Robert St. Louis of the state Conservation Department and was cleared by members of the ski club. This tow featured a wide-open slope with scattered trees and a view of Echo Lake. The vertical was 140 feet.

Snow trains would sometimes run to Amsterdam, about an hour's drive from Speculator, and a call to the Speculator Winter Sports Club would send a car to pick up skiers. Other nearby attractions for the Scribner Slope included a toboggan slide on Sturges Mountain, ice fishing and skating.

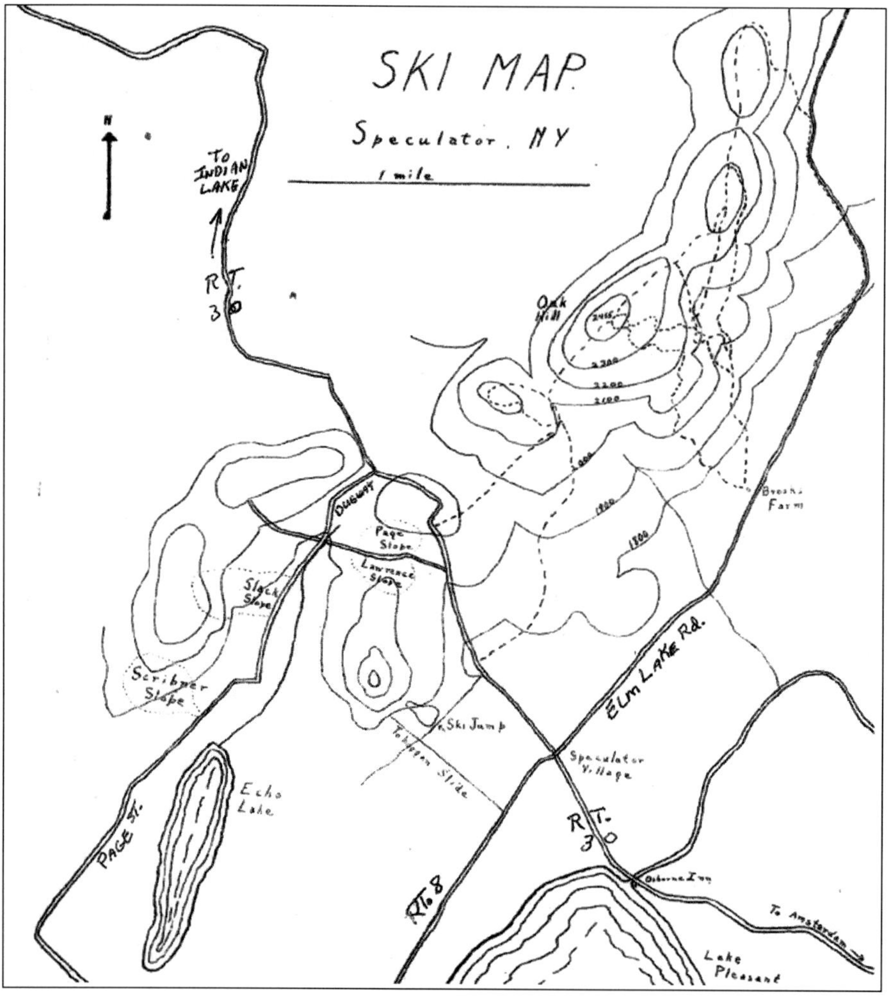

This map shows the various ski centers and slopes in Speculator prior to the operation of Oak Mountain. The Scribner Slope and Page Slope both boasted rope tows. The Slack Slope was often used for slalom races and was not lift served. The Lawrence Slope was not lift served either and was used for novices. A ski jump and toboggan slide were located a short distance southeast of these ski slopes. *Courtesy of the Historical Society of Lake Pleasant and Speculator.*

The Scribner Slope was popular and had a capacity for hundreds of skiers. The area continued to operate until the 1948–49 season. Then, the much larger Oak Mountain development, with its modern T-bar and quadruple the vertical drop, became the main game in town. Scribner closed, and its equipment was moved to Oak Mountain.

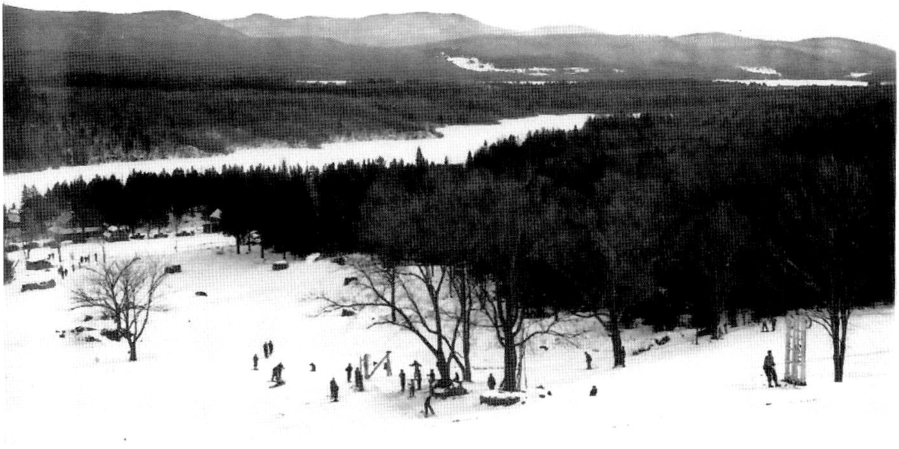

Scribner Slope, which had a rope tow, overlooked Echo Lake and had a beautiful view of surrounding mountains. Scattered trees provided interest to an otherwise open slope. Page Street can be seen at the lower left of the photo. *Courtesy of the Historical Society of Lake Pleasant and Speculator.*

Visiting the Area

The Scribner Slope is on private property. It has a few homes at the base and is otherwise forest with nothing to see. The exact location is nine-tenths of a mile south of the junction of Page Street and Dugway Road.

Page Hill at Melody Lodge

Speculator, New York

Late 1930s–49

The Melody Hill Lodge in Speculator briefly operated a rope tow for guests from the late 1930s into the late 1940s. Called Page Hill, the three-hundred-foot-long tow offered novices a chance to learn to ski on an easy slope. Bill Doremus, a ski instructor with a booming voice, taught lessons in 1939 before becoming a ski coach at Hamilton College. Tickets were $1.50 during the 1948–49 season, half the cost of the newly opened Oak Mountain. The opening of Oak Mountain, with a much larger complex of trails, resulted in the closing of this ski area in 1949. The tow was later removed and installed at Oak Mountain.

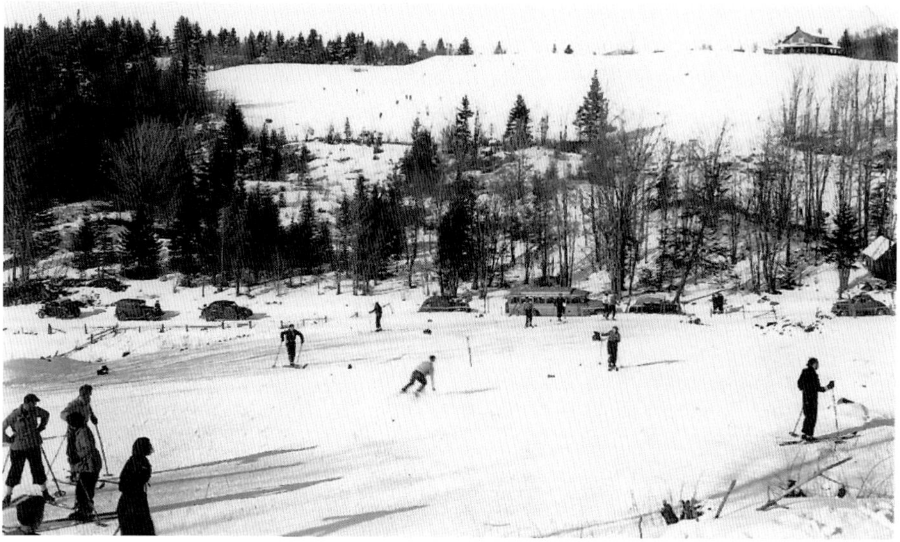

This view, taken from the Lawrence Slope, overlooked the Page Hill Slope in the background. The tow is not quite visible but was located below Melody Hill Lodge, which is seen at the top of the hill. Many beginners learned to ski at both the Lawrence Slope and Page Hill Slope. Today, the Page Hill Slope is still somewhat open, while the Lawrence Slope has seen home development along with reforestation. *Courtesy of the Historical Society of Lake Pleasant and Speculator.*

Visiting the Area

Melody Lodge continues to operate to this day and offers lodging and dining. The former ski slope at Melody Hill remains open with great views, but there are no other remnants of the ski center. For more information on the lodge, visit www.melodylodge.com.

Antler's Golf Course

Raquette Lake

Circa early 1950s

All three ski areas that once operated in Raquette Lake were brief operations, visited almost exclusively by local residents. None of the areas ever appeared in a ski guide, and none has any detailed documentation or exact dates of operation. Raquette Lake historian James Kammer showed the author all three locations of the tow, two of which are visible to the public.

The Antler's was a resort and golf course in the hamlet of Raquette Lake. The seventh hole was wide and smooth, with a decent drop. A rope tow was located alongside the slope for a few years in the early 1950s, and races were occasionally held on the slope. After a few years, the tow was moved to a more substantial hill on Brown Tract Road. The Antler's was sold and broken up in 1957, which resulted in the closure and redevelopment of the golf course.

Visiting the Area

The former golf course is hardly recognizable and is mostly on private land. The seventh hole, located off Antlers Road, has been redeveloped into private camps, with forest covering the rest of the slope. The area is not accessible to the public.

Brown's Tract Road Tow

Raquette Lake

Circa mid-1950s

Raquette Lake's rope was moved to Brown's Tract Road in the 1950s. This location was even farther away from the hamlet, which made access difficult in the wintertime. This tow was located on a larger and steeper hill than at Antler's and was used mostly for the annual winter carnival. The tow was moved to Mick's Hill, much closer to the center of the hamlet, at some point in the late 1950s.

Visiting the Area

The rope tow lift line is the most distinguishable feature of this former ski area. The slope has now completely returned to deep forest, making it hard to believe that a ski slope was ever in operation here. From the junction of Antlers Road and Brown's Tract Road just north of Raquette Lake, turn left onto Brown's Tract Road. Follow the road for exactly one mile. Directly in front of you will be the hill. When the leaves are off the trees, the rope towline can be visible on the right. You can continue driving around a curve to the top of the area to see the former unload section of the tow. No lift remnants are visible.

Special note: This road is not maintained for winter travel. Attempting to drive on this road in icy or snowy conditions could prove treacherous.

Mick's Hill

Raquette Lake

Circa late 1950s

The final location for Raquette Lake's tow was Mick's Hill, right in the hamlet. This was a short hill with one slope. It was a popular location for winter carnival activities. It closed due to liability costs and a lack of volunteers to run the tow.

Visiting the Area

Much of Mick's Hill has been developed into housing. However, a tiny, fifty-foot section of the rope tow lift line is still visible. This can be seen directly north of the junction of Church Road and Antlers Road. The rest of the slope is on private property.

Maple Ridge

Old Forge, New York

1936–92

Maple Ridge was one of the true pioneer ski centers in New York State. Open for non-lift-served skiing for the 1935–36 season, a rope tow was installed for the following year. Located directly in Old Forge, it attracted throngs of snow train visitors from the mid-1930s into the early 1940s, with additional snow trains from the mid-1940s into the mid-1950s. Skiing gradually shifted to the larger nearby McCauley Mountain beginning in

1958, leading to a slow decline in the use of Maple Ridge. By 1992, the area had closed for good.

Old Forge, a hamlet within the town of Webb, is truly one of the best locations in New York State for winter sports. A high elevation (1,700 feet above sea level), copious amounts of natural snow (about two hundred inches a year) and cold temperatures (New York's record low of fifty-two degrees below zero) all combine to set the stage for outdoor winter activities. Its earlier role as a popular summer resort, combined with good railroad access and roadways, helped ensure the development of winter sports in the 1930s.

Seeking to capitalize on the explosion of skiing in the mid-1930s, in 1935, the Old Forge Winter Sports Association constructed fourteen downhill trails throughout the region, from Bald Mountain to the north to McCauley Mountain outside of Old Forge. An open slope called Maple Ridge was developed adjacent to town on Park Avenue. In January 1936, a one-thousand-foot-long twisting toboggan slide was built next to the Maple Ridge slopes, which would provide thrills to skiers and non-skiers alike. It opened in early February.

On Sunday, January 19, 1936, the first snow train carrying nine hundred skiers and spectators from Syracuse and Utica arrived in nearby Thendara. Trucks, buses, dog sleds, taxis and private cars transported the skiers from Thendara, a mile away, to Old Forge. Some skiers made their own way, skiing across the former right of way of the old Fulton Chain Railroad, which led directly to the Maple Ridge slopes. The entire town celebrated their arrival with decorations and music. Skiers enjoyed the Maple Ridge slopes, a slalom slope behind the ridge, ice skating rink and other trails on nearby mountains. The snow train was a huge success, and seven more trains would follow on weekends for the rest of the season.

News of a new contraption, the rope tow, surely made its way to Old Forge during that winter. That same season, a rope tow was operational in North Creek and in several locations across New England. In December 1936, the Old Forge Hardware Company (still in business today) was granted a lease to build a rope tow at Maple Ridge. It had rented out skis and toboggans to snow train visitors the previous year. A seven-hundred-foot-long ski tow was hastily constructed in late December, which allowed skiers an easier way to reach the summit of Maple Ridge. It would be extended by three hundred feet the following winter.

Max Bolli, a famous Swiss ski instructor, taught skiing at Maple Ridge from 1937 through 1956, with a several-year gap in the late 1940s and early

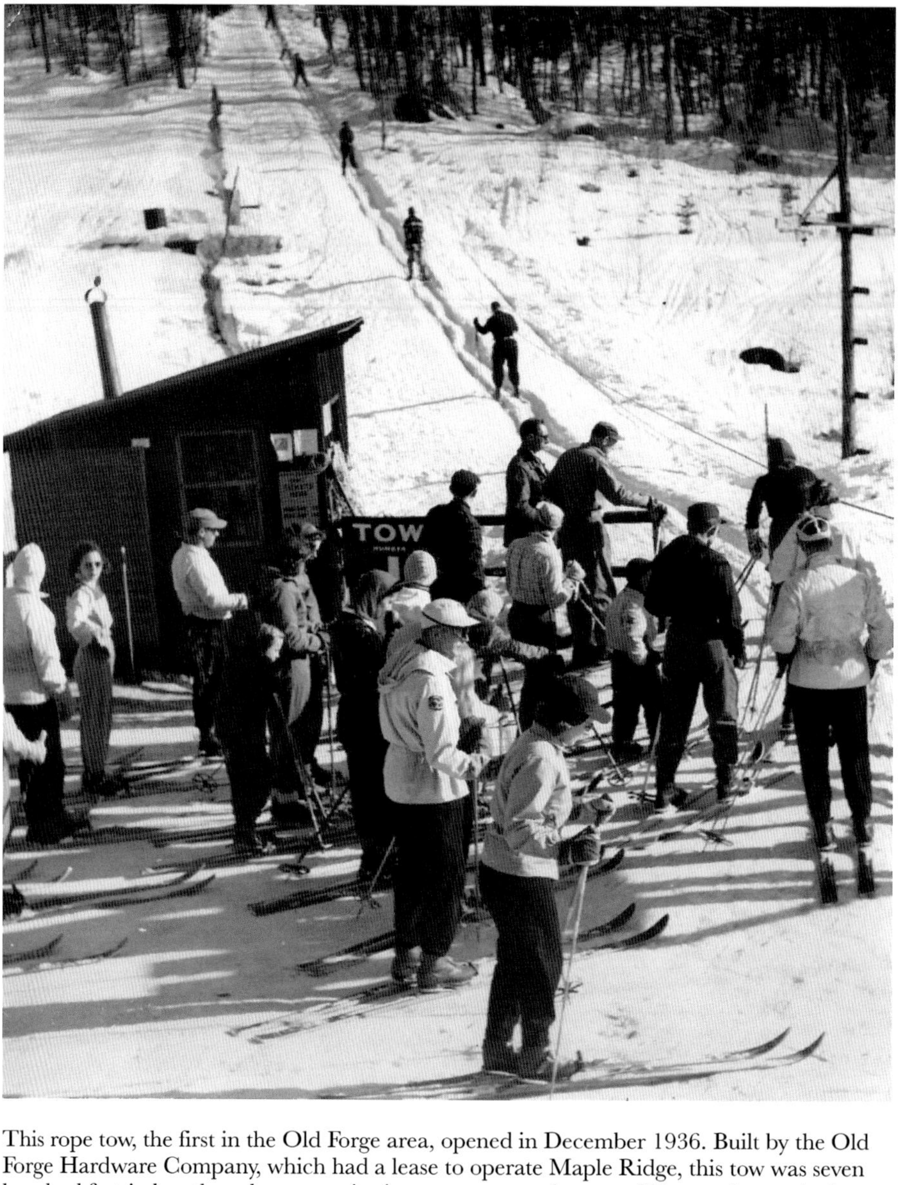

This rope tow, the first in the Old Forge area, opened in December 1936. Built by the Old Forge Hardware Company, which had a lease to operate Maple Ridge, this tow was seven hundred feet in length and was a major improvement to the area. Skiers no longer had to hike up the slope under their own power. A T-bar lift was constructed at Maple Ridge in 1959, which eventually led to this rope tow being abandoned. *Courtesy of the Town of Webb Historical Association.*

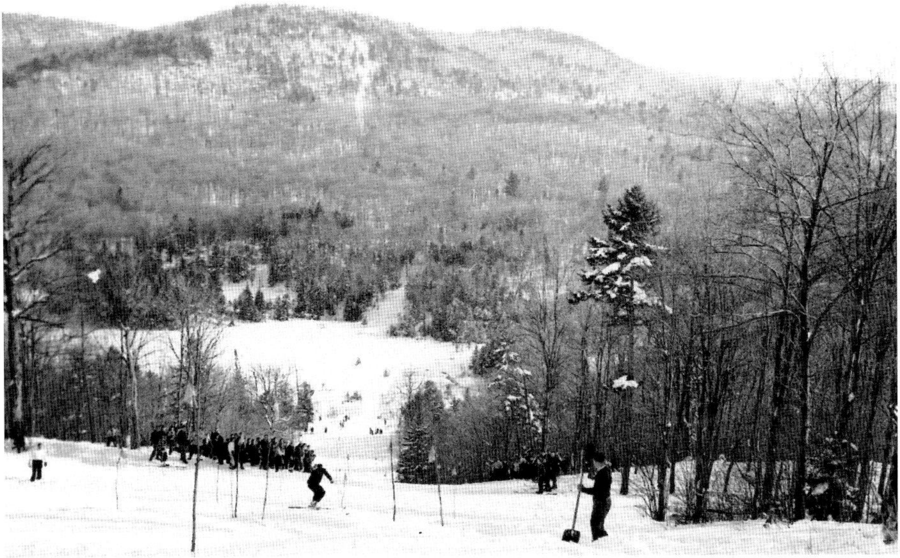

The Hell-Gate Slalom Slope at Maple Ridge was solely for experts and for racing events. Located on the back side of Maple Ridge and down toward Gray Lake, the slope was accessed by an 850-foot-long rope tow, which led from the summit of Maple Ridge. Skiers would have to hike back up the slope, which reduced its popularity. By the early to mid-1950s, this isolated slope was abandoned, and it is mostly reforested today. The rope tow engine can still be found near the summit. McCauley Mountain, in the background, was not lift served at this point, but the DeCamp Trail, accessed by hiking only, can be seen. *Courtesy of the Town of Webb Historical Association.*

1950s due to a car accident. He had skied from Syracuse to Lake Placid in 1931, a 175-mile trip! Many snow train passengers and locals alike learned to ski from Bolli.

Throughout the late 1930s and into the early 1940s, Maple Ridge continued to be a very popular destination. Snow trains and buses, often carrying between five hundred and one thousand skiers from the Utica/Syracuse area, jammed the slopes. When skiing was limited elsewhere in the state, there was almost always skiing in Old Forge. The slopes were also illuminated at night.

While World War II diminished skiing at Maple Ridge, it would rebound in 1946. The snow trains gradually came to an end and were completely finished in 1954, as more and more skiers were able to afford automobiles and drive themselves to Old Forge.

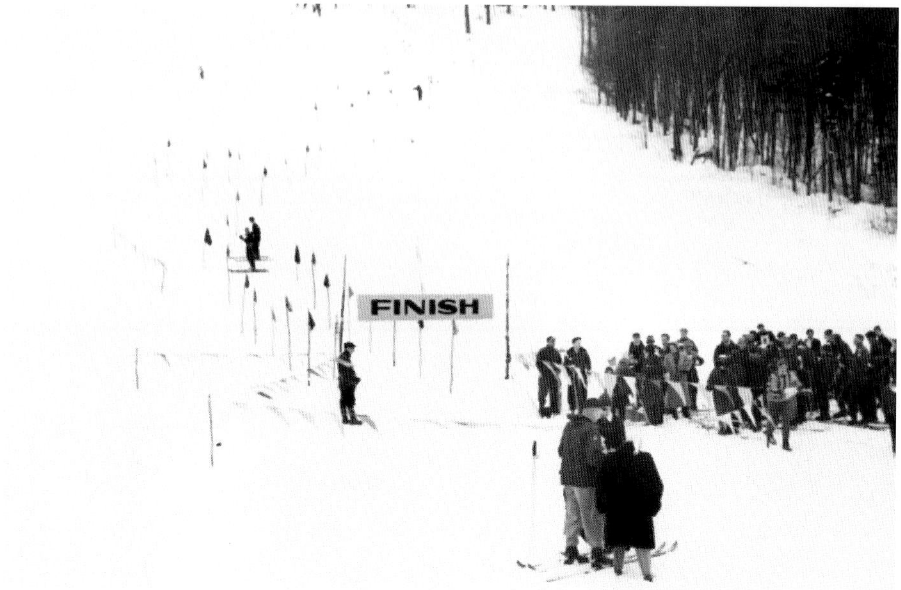

Alpine Slope, located just to the southwest of Maple Ridge, was often used for racing events. Opened in the late 1940s, this slope complemented Maple Ridge and featured a 1,200-foot-long rope tow, located just to the left of this view. Scattered trees near the top of the slope added interest for more advanced skiers. Alpine Ridge was abandoned in the mid-1970s due to declining use. Today, it is all forest, save for the rope tow lift line, which is still clear. *Courtesy of the Town of Webb Historical Association.*

Major improvements would come to Maple Ridge throughout the 1940s. Two new rope tows were built: one from the top of the first tow to carry skiers across a relatively flat section at the summit and another tow up the steep slalom slope on the backside in 1947. Called the Hell-Gate Slalom, this steep trail provided many thrills and a beautiful view of McCauley Mountain. Jim Ehrensbeck remembers this slalom slope as being extremely fast. He remembers watching one skier who flew down the slope in about twenty-six seconds! The slalom slope and tow would continue to operate into the 1950s before being abandoned.

Another slope next to Maple Ridge was partially cleared before World War II. Called Alpine Slope, a new 1,200-foot-long rope tow was also built around 1947. Alpine provided an overflow slope for Maple Ridge, reducing pressure on its rope tow. The upper portions of Alpine had scattered trees, and the rest of the slope was often used for racing as well. The slope was in use until the early 1970s before being abandoned.

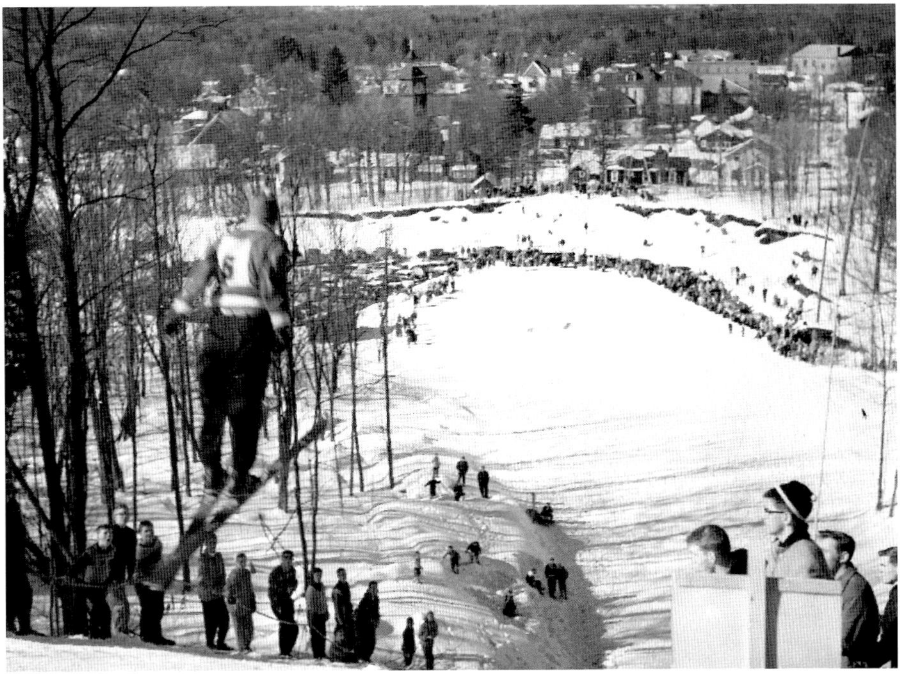

The forty-meter jump located adjacent to Maple Ridge was the site of many competitions and exhibitions. Here, a jumper wows the large crowd gathered below, with a view of Old Forge in the background. Once popular, ski jump events faded in popularity, and by the 1960s, this jump was abandoned. Today, this location is in the woods and can be visited via a hiking trail. *Courtesy of the Town of Webb Historical Association.*

A forty-meter ski jump was built at Maple Ridge in 1954. Located a short distance north of the slope, jumpers would thrill huge crowds of spectators that gathered at the bottom. A smaller jump was constructed on the south side of Maple Ridge a year later, used as practice before jumpers took to the main jump. Winter carnivals were also quite popular, with many events for skiers and children.

After Max Bolli retired from ski instructing at Maple Ridge, Jim Ehrensbeck took over the Old Forge Ski School and the Town of Webb School at Maple Ridge from 1946 until about 1950, continuing to instruct using the Swiss technique. He had learned to ski from Bolli in the 1930s. Ehrensbeck left to teach at the Concord Hotel and was replaced by Bolli again in 1952. Ehrensbeck would later become the manager at McCauley Mountain for many years and had a long career with Hall Ski Lifts, installing numerous ski areas throughout the country.

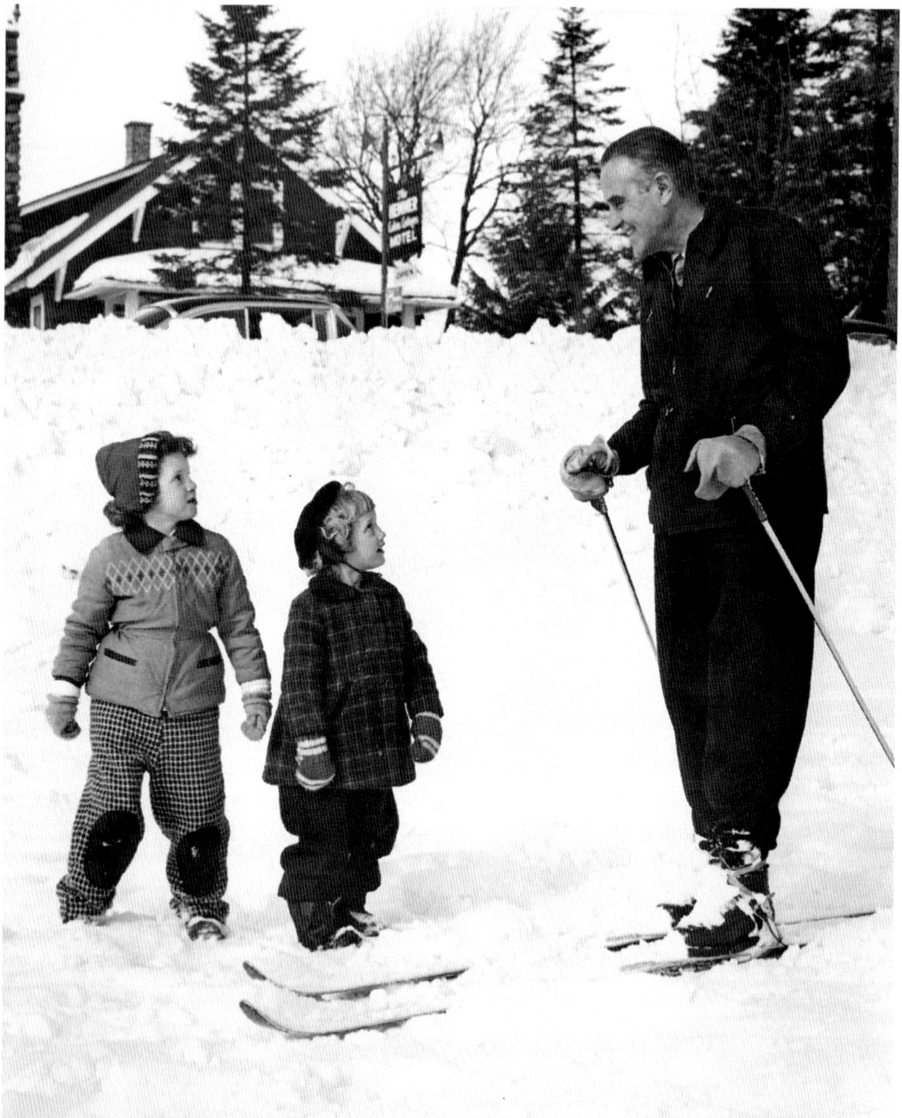

Old Forge Winter Carnivals, organized by the Polar Bear Club and Old Forge Winter Sports Association, attracted winter sports enthusiasts from all across the Adirondacks to the Utica area. Even Governor W. Averell Harriman, who founded Sun Valley, Idaho, visited the carnival at Maple Ridge and took the time to meet with these young skiers. *Courtesy of the Town of Webb Historical Association.*

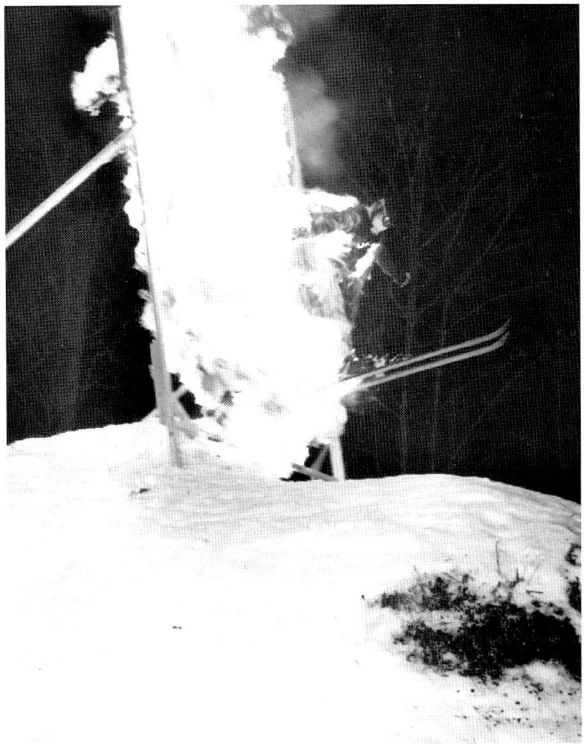

The annual Old Forge Winter Carnival was held for many years at Maple Ridge and featured ski races, fireworks and a torchlight parade. Daredevil stunts were also performed. Here, Norm Villiere, a ski instructor, manager and all-around expert skier at Maple Ridge, thrills the crowd by jumping through a hoop of fire. Almost all Town of Webb ski students participated in the torchlight parades and stunts at the carnival. *Courtesy of the Town of Webb Historical Association.*

In 1956, Norm Villiere took over the ski school and became very popular. He would also perform stunts at the annual winter carnival, including one where he jumped through a hoop of fire. He was also the manager of Maple Ridge in the 1960s and taught skiing at McCauley as well. One skier at Maple Ridge remembers, "I always tried to stay in beginner's class because in the intermediate classes, Norm would teach jumping and other stunts [such as jumping through fire hoops]."

Much of the effort in operating Maple Ridge during this time was done by volunteers, with a lot of the operating expenses being raised through fundraisers. The Old Forge Winter Sports Association held various fundraisers in the summer that would be plowed back into improvements at the ski area.

For the 1958–59 ski season, major changes that would greatly impact the future of Maple Ridge were felt. First, McCauley Mountain Ski Area, a much larger operation with modern lifts, was built just behind Maple Ridge. Featuring a vertical drop of about six hundred feet, along with a modern T-bar (one of the first built by Hall Ski Lifts), it gave local and regional ski areas a larger

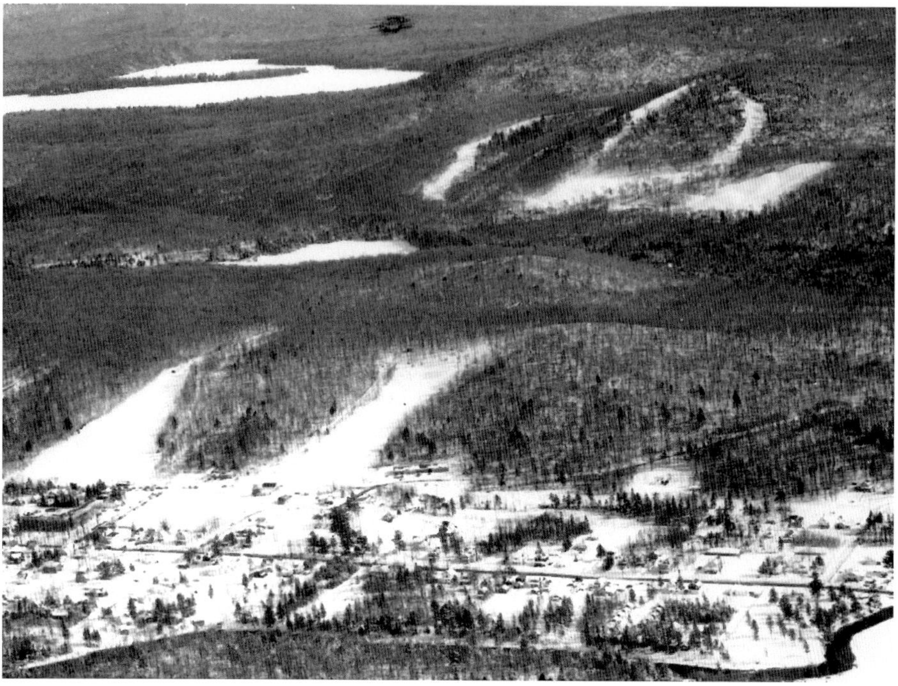

A very late 1950s or early 1960s aerial view shows the variety of skiing available in Old Forge. At the bottom left is Maple Ridge, and to its immediate right is Alpine Slope. Above and to the right is the new ski center of McCauley Mountain, which continues to operate to this day. Not seen in this image is the Hell-Gate Slalom Slope, which had declined in usage at that time and dropped from the backside of Maple Ridge toward McCauley Mountain. *Courtesy of the Town of Webb Historical Association.*

alternative to Maple Ridge. The gradual shifting of skiing from Maple Ridge to McCauley would result in a slow decline for the ski area.

Even with McCauley opening, voters approved a measure to improve the facilities at Maple Ridge. Snow making was installed in 1958, using Larchmont snow guns. For 1960, a $25,000 T-bar was built right up the center of Maple Ridge, which would eventually lead to the closing of the rope tow, though the tow that year was replaced with an electric engine. This T-bar made access to the slope significantly easier, and Maple Ridge became more of a training center for residents and children as opposed to a destination area as it had been in its snow train days. It is believed that the snow-making operation only ran for a few years, and a lack of a snow-making pond or water source, along with high natural snowfalls, rendered the snow-making system unnecessary.

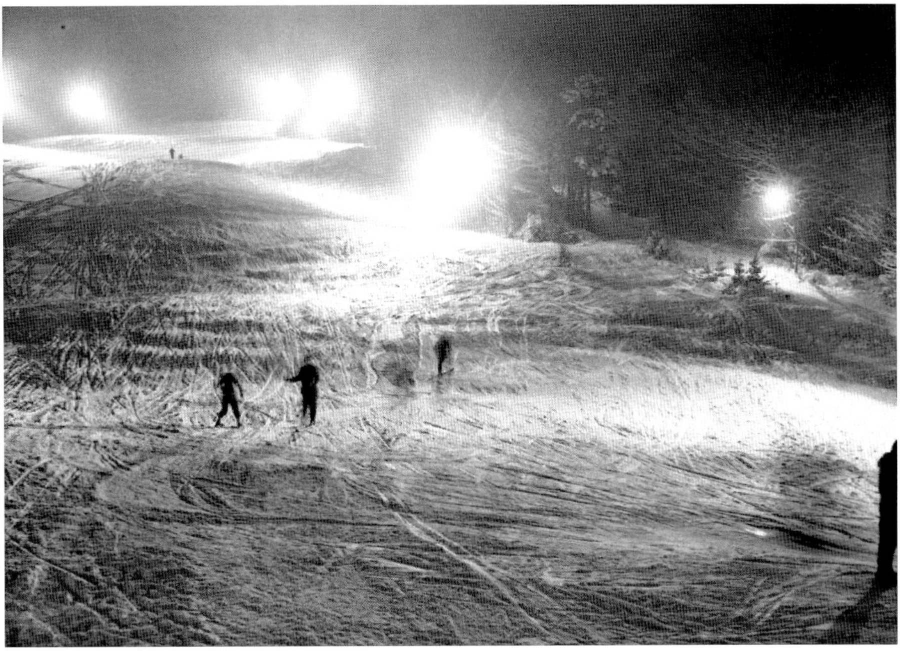

In 1958, lights for night skiing were installed as part of a major improvement project at Maple Ridge. Bright illumination allowed skiers the chance to enjoy the sport after work. These skiers were certainly enjoying the fresh powder under the lights. Note the rope tow on the right, which was also lit. A few light sockets can still be found on the trees today. *Courtesy of the Town of Webb Historical Association.*

In the 1960s, Maple Ridge was a true family ski area geared mainly toward children. William Bishop III, who skied here during that time, remembers, "Back then, the lift operators knew everybody. The place would be packed with local kids on weekends and especially weekdays after school let out. It was the community place for local kids and families to hang out and have fun."

By the 1980s, snowfalls had begun to become more inconsistent at the ski area, and schoolchildren were more and more frequently using McCauley Mountain with its superior facilities. The 1991–92 season would prove to be the final one of operation at Maple Ridge, opening for only three or four days. The town board and board of education decided to halt operations in 1992 and move the program to McCauley Mountain. The T-bar stood on the slope until the early 2000s and then was mostly dismantled, though the summit return station remains. Trees are beginning to grow on the slope. Despite the loss of skiing at Maple Ridge, McCauley continues to offers

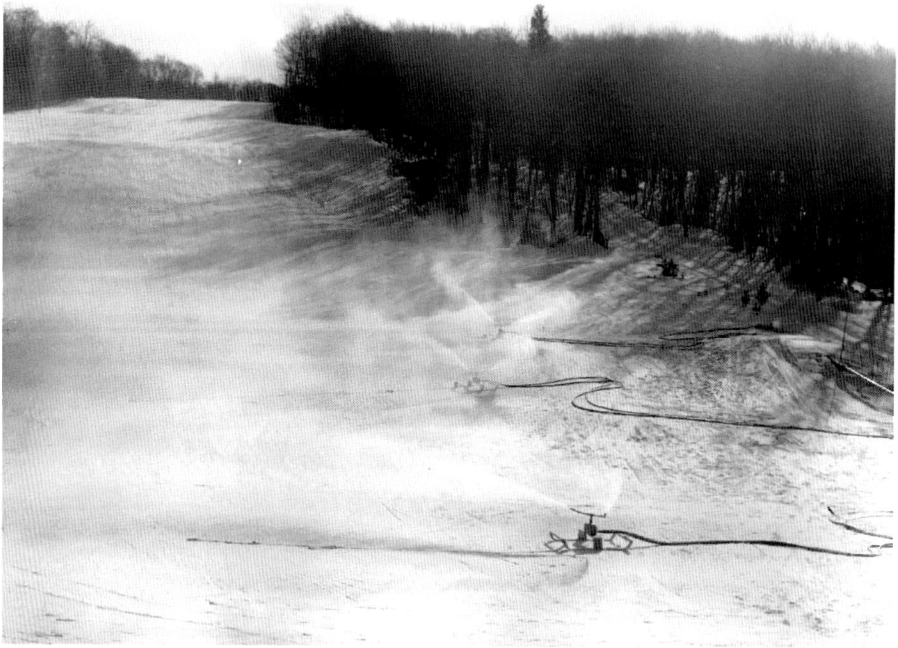

For a time, snow making was a feature at Maple Ridge. Installed with other improvements in 1958 by the Larchmont Company, these snow-making nozzles were able to provide man-made snow when natural snow was not available. Snow making did not make a permanent appearance at Maple Ridge and was likely only available until the early 1960s. Frequent natural snowfalls and an increasing focus of development at McCauley Mountain resulted in the removal of the snow-making equipment. *Courtesy of the Town of Webb Historical Association.*

locals and visitors a classic Adirondack ski experience, with affordable rates, a variety of trails and usually plenty of snow. In addition, skiers on the trails can also look across Gray Lake and just make out the former slalom slope across the lake, almost now indistinguishable from the surrounding woods.

The legacy of Maple Ridge is vast. Three skiers who learned at the area went on to the Olympics. One, Gary Vaughn, was on the U.S. Olympic Alpine Team in 1959 but got bumped at the finale cut. He later coached the Dartmouth Ski Team. John "Louie" Ehrensbeck was a biathlon participant in the 1964 Olympics and was also on the Alpine Ski Team for several years. Finally, Hank Kashiwa Jr. was on the 1972 Alpine Ski Team at Sapporo. He had a successful career as a skiing commentator, founded the Volant Ski Corporation and has been inducted into the Colorado Ski Hall of Fame. Smaller ski areas like Maple Ridge produce big results!

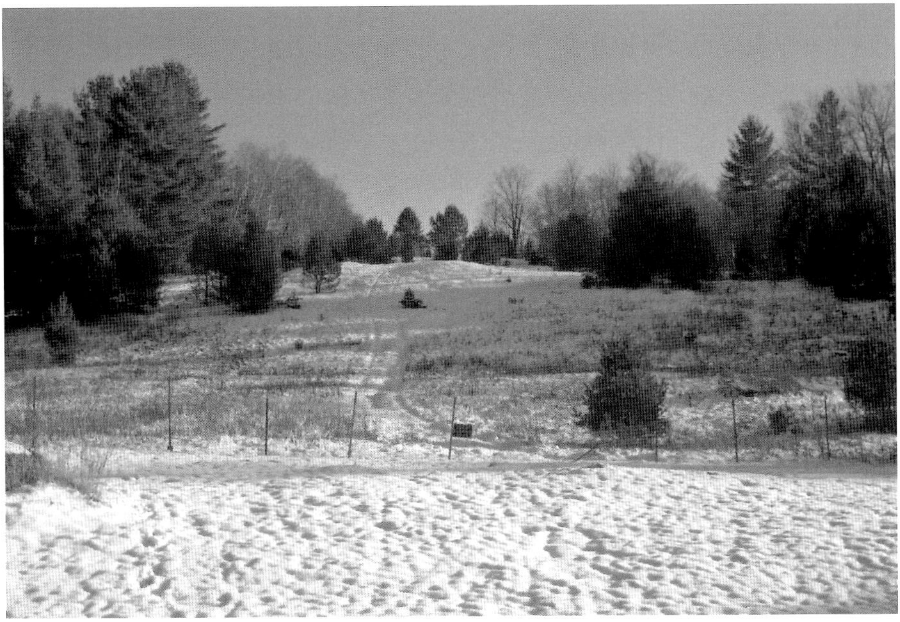

In 2011, Maple Ridge continues the process of succession, slowly returning to nature. Pine trees are beginning to grow on the slopes where thousands of children (and adults) learned to ski. A hiking trail is still accessible on this slope, which is closed to skiing or sledding. Unless the slope is mowed or cleared, within ten to fifteen years it will be difficult to ever know there was a ski area here.

Visiting the Area

If you are planning to explore Maple Ridge, you will definitely want to give yourself plenty of time—at least a full morning or afternoon. There is quite a lot to explore in all seasons.

The complex is located just behind the school on Park Avenue in Old Forge, with plenty of paved parking at the base of the former ski area. The former ski area will be right in front of you, with sparsely spaced trees growing on the open slope. From the parking lot, walk northeast for about a minute to a kiosk that displays all the various trails at Maple Ridge. Locations for the former ski jump, toboggan chute, ski trails and lift remnants are clearly displayed. Trail maps can sometimes be obtained at the kiosk or can be printed online at oldforgeny.com/recreation.html.

Use the map to follow the trails to visit the former ski jump, about a ten-minute hike from the kiosk. You cannot miss the steep plunge where jumpers used to land at dizzying speed. The wooden jump, however, has been long removed, with no trace remaining except for a small clearing.

The former slalom run is also marked on the trail map; it has become reforested but is still recognizable. You will also see the remains of the former rope tow that served this slope at the top of the slope.

At the top of the former Maple Ridge slope, remnants of the former T-bar, including the return station, are still standing. Just below the water tower is the lift line for the rope tow, which remains clear and open today; however, there are no remnants of this lift. Enjoy the views of Old Forge from the top of the lost ski area.

The Alpine Slope, part of the complex, is located just southwest of Maple Ridge behind a town garage. This slope has transitioned to woods and is barely recognizable. Parts of the rope towline of this ski area remain clear, but there is little else to see at Alpine.

A visit to the Town of Webb Historical Association's Goodsell Museum in Old Forge is not to be missed, as it has many archives and displays of winter sports history, including those at Maple Ridge. Visit webbhistory.org for more information.

Chapter 5
Restored Ski Areas

Four formerly lost ski areas have been restored in the last decade. In order to be considered "restored," these ski areas had to have been closed for a decade or more. Some ski areas, like Oak Mountain or Hickory Ski Center, had closed for a few years at some point in their existence but are open and fully operational today. As their closing periods were relatively brief, they are not included in this chapter.

All four of these areas had been abandoned in some way, either left with rusting ski lifts in place (such as the North Creek Ski Bowl) or becoming reforested (such as Darrow's). Two of them—the North Creek Ski Bowl and the Schroon Lake Ski Center—are open to the public, with the latter having free skiing available for all. Darrow's and Schaefer Skiland are privately owned and operated for friends and family only.

It is unlikely that other lost ski areas will become restored, though it is not impossible. Little Alpine in Remsen may offer lift-served tubing in the future, but almost all other areas have such significant hurdles to reopening that it is highly improbable that they will come back.

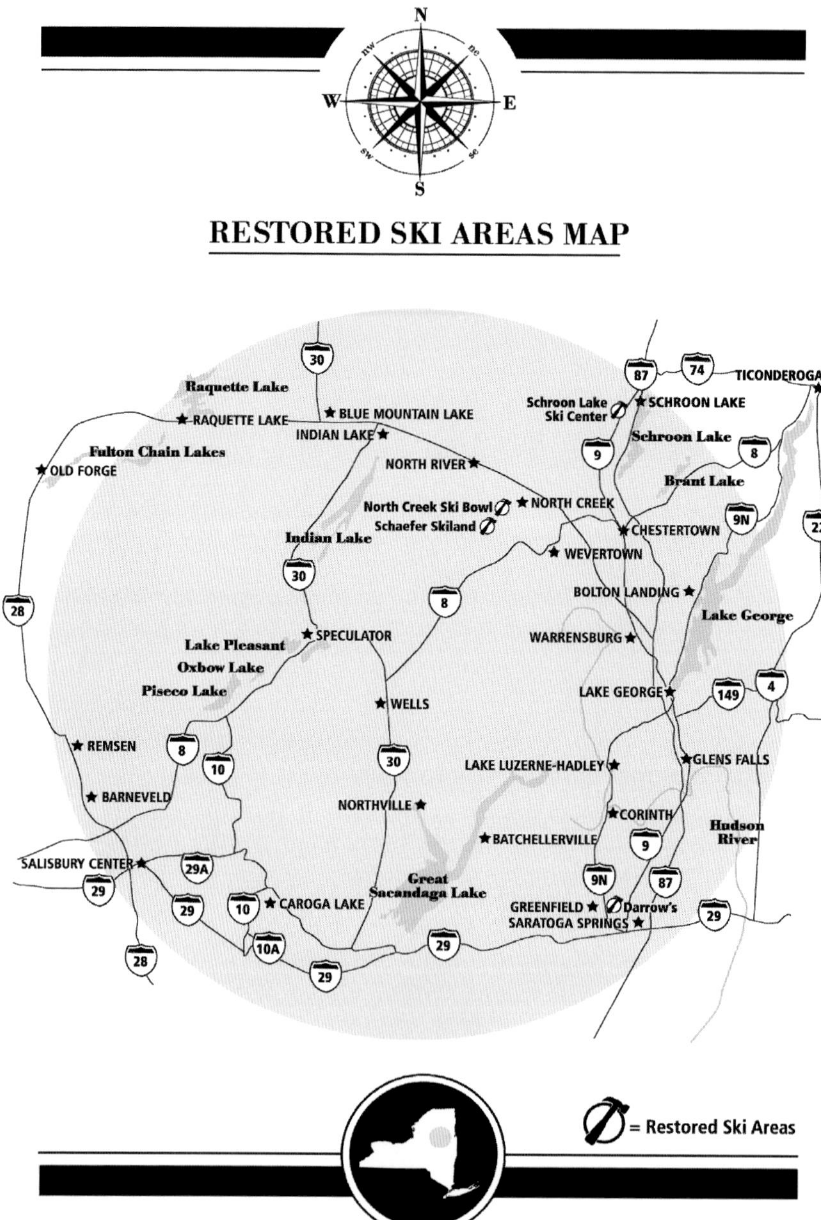

Four former lost ski areas have now been restored. The North Creek Ski Bowl and Schroon Lake Ski Center are open to the public, while Darrow's and Schaefer Skiland are private. It is doubtful that any other lost ski areas will reopen in the future. *Map designed by Scott Cahill.*

Darrow's

Greenfield, New York

1939–68, 2010–present

After the attempt to operate Sisto's Farm as a ski area in South Corinth failed, Ed Taylor Jr. scouted out another suitable location for a ski area. Earl Darrow's Farm off Locust Grove Road in Greenfield had been previously used as an open slope with no lift. Taylor found the slope to be wide, smooth and consistent, with a summit elevation of nearly seven hundred feet. The hill had an expansive view of the Upper Hudson Valley and east into Vermont. An east-facing slope also protected the area against stronger afternoon sunshine. In addition, the farm was located only about ten minutes from downtown Saratoga Springs.

Taylor secured a lease with Darrow, operating the ski center on his property in exchange for 10 percent of the profits. The tow opened in 1939, just prior to the Skidmore Winter Carnival, which was held at the ski area. Lights were installed for night skiing, and the area was an instant success. Cattle grazed the slopes during the summer months, helping to keep brush to a minimum.

Darrow's was operated by Taylor into the early 1940s, and Skidmore College students were frequently at Darrow's and were taught by the expert Taylor. It is unknown if the ski center operated during World War II, but by 1944, Taylor had moved on to found Alpine Meadows a few miles north.

It is not clear who operated the ski area during the rest of the 1940s, but by the early 1950s, Tommy Orton became the owner of the ski area. His friend Larry Mahar and others were invited to join the partnership. Mahar describes operating the tow, which could be tricky to ride:

> *The area had only one rope tow driven by an old automobile engine pulling the rope. It had an automatic emergency shut-off on top of the hill to prevent skiers who didn't let go of the rope from being pulled into the engine. It consisted of a "hit string," which anyone who went past the safe point would hit and disengage the engine. I and one of the other owners would take turns standing watch at skiers as they engaged the rope at the bottom of the hill and exited it at the top of the hill. The owners kept careful watch of people, especially youngsters, engaging the rope at the bottom of the hill because the beginning skiers had a penchant of tumbling as they grabbed the moving rope.*

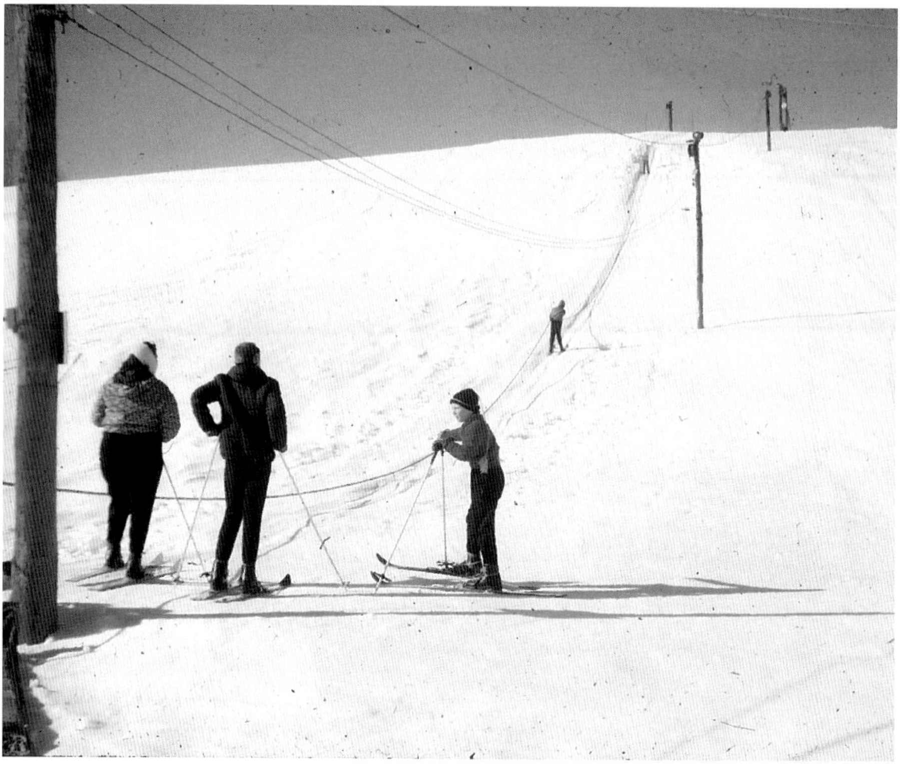

Throughout the early existence of Darrow's, a five-hundred-foot rope tow brought skiers to the top of a one-hundred-foot vertical slope. Skiers had the option of a steeper southern slope or a more gradual northern slope. There were no trails, as the ski area operated on a farm. Lights for night skiing can be seen mounted next to the rope tow. *Courtesy of Bill Bennett.*

There were many ups and downs with operating Darrow's, with variable snowfalls and never much income. Mahar describes the challenges:

> *There were good years and bad years. A bad year would see as little as thirteen days of skiable snow. A good year would be much longer. The only advertising the ski area got was a sign at the end of the road which connected with a main highway. My friend Tom and I were the only owners who actually skied. A typical season showed little or no profits after buying the new rope needed each year, the insurance and the lease which was 10 percent of gross sales.*

Due to these challenges, the ski operation was sold, this time to Ron Strader and Ray Bennett in 1957. Their new operation opened for their first season on January 11, 1958, and continued through March 16. They would operate the area through the 1959–60 season, before Bennett left the operation, and was replaced by his brother Jimmy. Incidentally, their brother Bill was a frequent skier at Darrow's and would later head the ski school at Alpine Meadows. The Bennetts and Strader very much enjoyed running Darrow's, though it never made them much money. The busiest day at Darrow's was March 6, 1960, when fifty skiers packed the slopes.

Improvements were made to the area, including a warming hut that was built using boards from a former hotel that was being demolished on South Broadway in Saratoga Springs. Strader and Bennett also removed from the hotel four plate-glass windows, which were then installed in the new warming hut. Anna Mae Bennett, the mother of the Bennett brothers, volunteered her time to operate the warming hut, serving hot chocolate, homemade cookies and hot dogs. Whenever a child was having a problem on the slope or was cold and tired, he would be sent to the warming hut, where Anna Mae would assist him.

Other additions to the hill included classical music that was piped out across the slopes, and in 1962, a short beginner rope tow was installed a short distance away from the main tow.

Throughout the 1960s, Skidmore College students continued to use the slope as a learning hill, with lessons offered through the school. Coach Ron Farra also brought the Saratoga High School ski team to Darrow's to practice on occasion in the mid-1960s.

Plans were being developed at the new Skidmore College campus to have its own ski area, and in 1968, skiing at Darrow's came to an end. The tow was sold to the college, which operated it for a few years before being replaced by a modern T-bar. A few rope tow towers can still be seen at the base of the former area at Skidmore.

With the departure of the rope tow, Darrow's was left to grow in, becoming a tangle of brush and trees. The property was later purchased by Carter Yepsen, who built a home at the top of the old ski area. He wanted to reactivate the ski area in his backyard. He purchased a used handle tow from Sugarloaf in Maine, and a volunteer crew helped clear a new slope and gladed section in the fall of 2010. While the hill is still significantly reforested as compared to its past, it now offers a variety of skiing on a one-hundred-foot vertical drop. The handle tow is now in operation, but only for family and friends, as this is a private area.

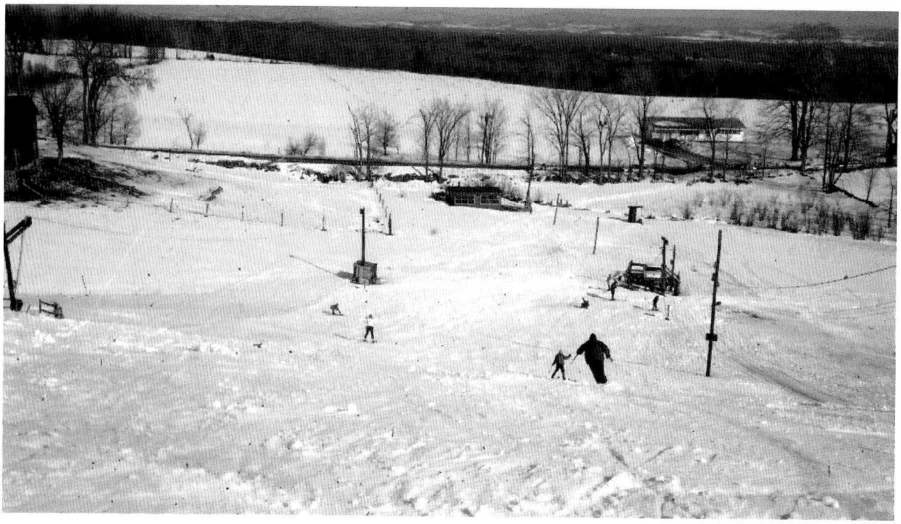

For the 1962–63 ski season, a beginner rope tow was added to Darrow's, as depicted here on the left. The original rope tow is located on the right. The warming hut is also visible, located just off Locust Grove Road. A beautiful vista to the east, including the hills of Washington County and the mountains of Vermont, can be seen. *Courtesy of Ron and Arlene Strader.*

Visiting the Area

Darrow's is on private property, but the ski area can be seen on Locust Grove Road. From the railroad crossing on Locust Grove Road, head north for just under six-tenths of a mile. The ski area will be visible on the hillside on the left.

North Creek Ski Bowl, "Old Gore"

North Creek, New York

1947–71, 1972–early 2000s, 2007–present

The North Creek Ski Bowl is certainly an interesting and unique restored area. Built with the fusion of new terrain and the Village Slope terrain, this major ski area was popular from the late 1940s into the 1960s, when Gore Mountain opened. In the late 1970s, the main lift closed, but a shorter T-bar continued to operate, making the area a hybrid of lost and open. It has since been restored and merged into the Gore Mountain Ski Area, and has a promising future.

In 1946, the assets of the Village Slopes were sold to a new partnership of the Gore Mountain Ski Club and investors. Called the Gore Mountain Ski Corporation, its primary objective was to offer increased lift-served skiing in the region. A 3,200-foot-long electric Constam T-bar was installed, along with several new trails. The vertical drop was increased to nearly 900 feet, and additional trails were constructed. Some utilized parts of older trails from the "ride up, slide down" days.

One of the new trails was the Hudson. An expert run, it steeply dropped from the summit with several difficult turns. The Ridge Trail was intermediate and connected into the old Slalom Slope area that used to have a rope tow. The ski hut and rope tows on the Open Slope from the previous operation were included into the operation. The T-bar opened in January 1947 and was well received.

The Ski Bowl remained a popular location in the late 1940s and into the 1950s. The Constam T-bar was a dramatic improvement over the earlier rope tows, and the variety of terrain kept skiers happy.

Skiing almost came to an end at the Ski Bowl in 1958. Friction had been building between the lift corporation and the town. The corporation did not have the necessary funds to maintain the T-bar, and opposition from other hamlets in the town of Johnsburg was increasing. Four out of the five hamlets felt that they were receiving no benefit from the subsidization of the ski area. Thankfully, the problem was resolved, and the ski area did open for the season.

Changes came to the ski school in the late 1950s. Olympian Dot Hoyt Nebel had been teaching at the Ski Bowl, but she left to teach at Oak Mountain for 1959, leaving it with no instructor. Don Petro, a self-taught skier who had studied the Austrian method, became a very popular instructor. He shortly became a certified instructor and would increase the staff and have ten instructors working under him at one time. Private lessons were available for eight dollars, with group lessons costing skiers three dollars. In 1968, Petro left the Ski Bowl after some disagreement with the owners and became the ski school director at Jiminy Peak in Massachusetts.

The opening of Gore Mountain for the 1963–64 ski season resulted in a sea change for the North Creek area and was a double-edged sword. A lot of skiers skied at Gore, but on busy days, the Ski Bowl would receive overflow traffic. During the 1960s, the Ski Bowl advertised the lack of lift lines and uncrowded skiing, and for a time, it worked.

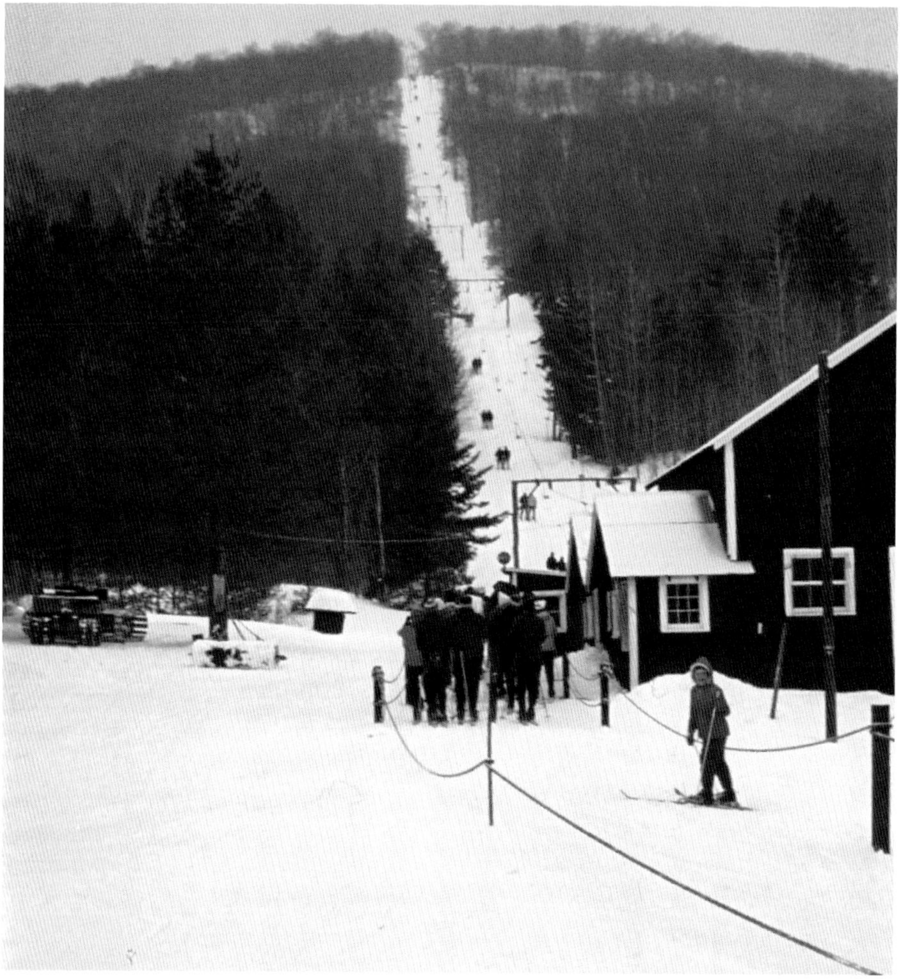

The North Creek Ski Bowl T-bar allowed skiers to access nearly nine hundred vertical feet of classic New York skiing. One of the first major ski lifts in the state, the lift operated until the late 1970s, when it was abandoned. The lift line was dramatically widened and reopened with a refurbished triple chairlift in January 2011. *Courtesy of Larry Wilke.*

Improvements came to the Ski Bowl for the 1964–65 season when the two rope tows were replaced by a modern T-bar. This allowed for easier access to the top of the Open Slope, an ideal teaching slope. This tow was purchased and leased by the Town of Johnsburg and would operate long after the main T-bar had closed.

In 1968, the lift corporation sold the assets to Kay Gifford, the former manager at Oak Mountain in Speculator. She was a pioneer in the ski

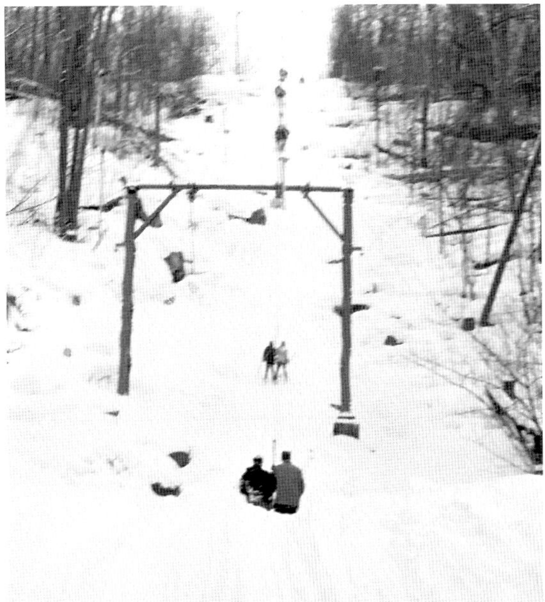

Upper portions of the North Creek Ski Bowl T-bar, shown here in the 1960s, featured a very steep incline. Lighter skiers, particularly children, could find themselves nearly airborne on this section. Skiers could exit off to the right at this point to avoid the tough pitch ahead. *Courtesy of Larry Wilke.*

industry, as there were few female ski area managers or owners in the 1960s. The competition from Gore Mountain took its toll, and the Ski Bowl closed at the end of the 1970–71 ski season. Gifford then sold the ski area to Burger Enterprises, founded by Elting Q. Burger, who was an architect, engineer and teacher. The ski area promptly reopened in January 1972. Joel Beaudin was appointed the manager. The beginner T-bar was leased from the Town of Johnsburg.

Plans were drawn up to add a double chairlift to the right of the T-bar, add trails and snow making and double the size of the base lodge, but this was not to be. The ski area continued to operate until about 1977, when Burger Enterprises folded. The main T-bar to the summit was left in place, where it decayed, and trees sprouted on the majority of the trails. The base lodge burned to the ground, leaving only the fireplace standing. Plans came and went to redevelop the mountain into a four-season resort, but these all failed.

Despite the loss of the main mountain, the beginner T-bar continued to operate, sometimes sporadically, under the Town of Johnsburg until the early 2000s. During this period, the T-bar was open mostly on weekends and holidays and was used almost exclusively by children in town. At some point in the early 2000s, the T-bar ceased operation, and a fire destroyed the lift building for the older main lift.

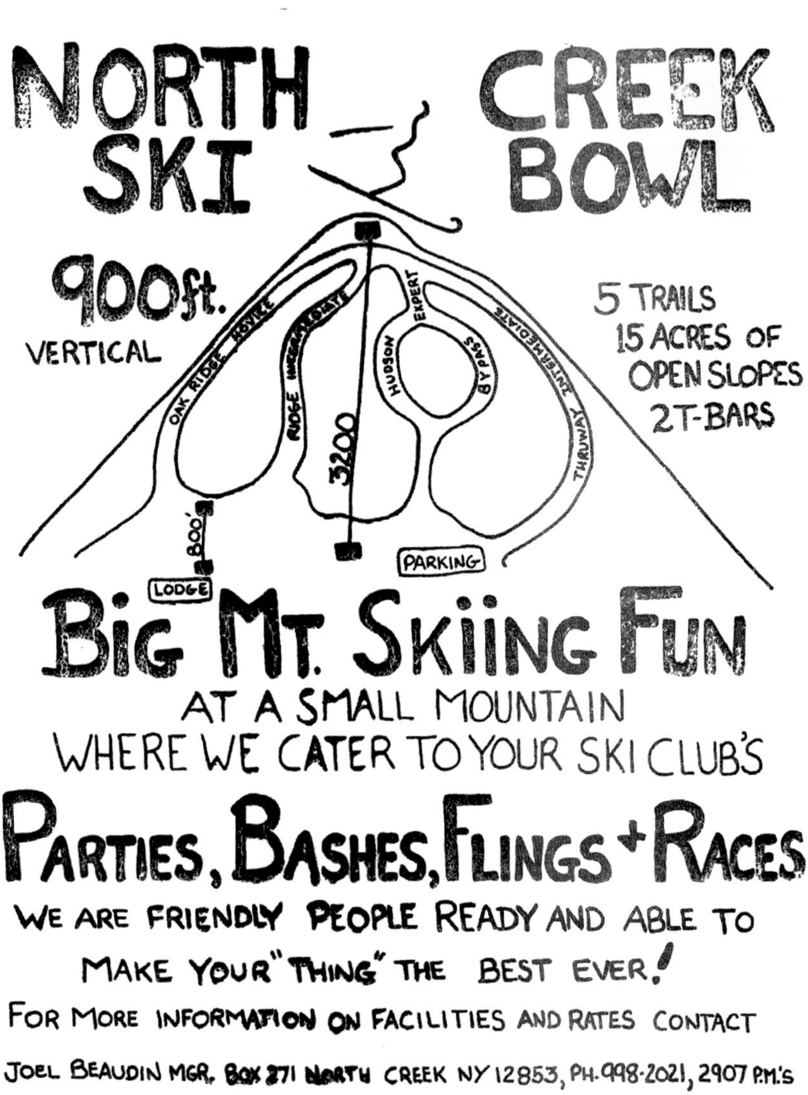

This flyer was found by the author inside the former lift house for the original North Creek T-bar in 2001. Likely dating from 1977, the flyer promoted the benefits of ski clubs hosting their events at the mountain. The last trail map for the Ski Bowl was included as well. It was a good thing the flyer was rescued; a few years later, the lift building was destroyed by arson.

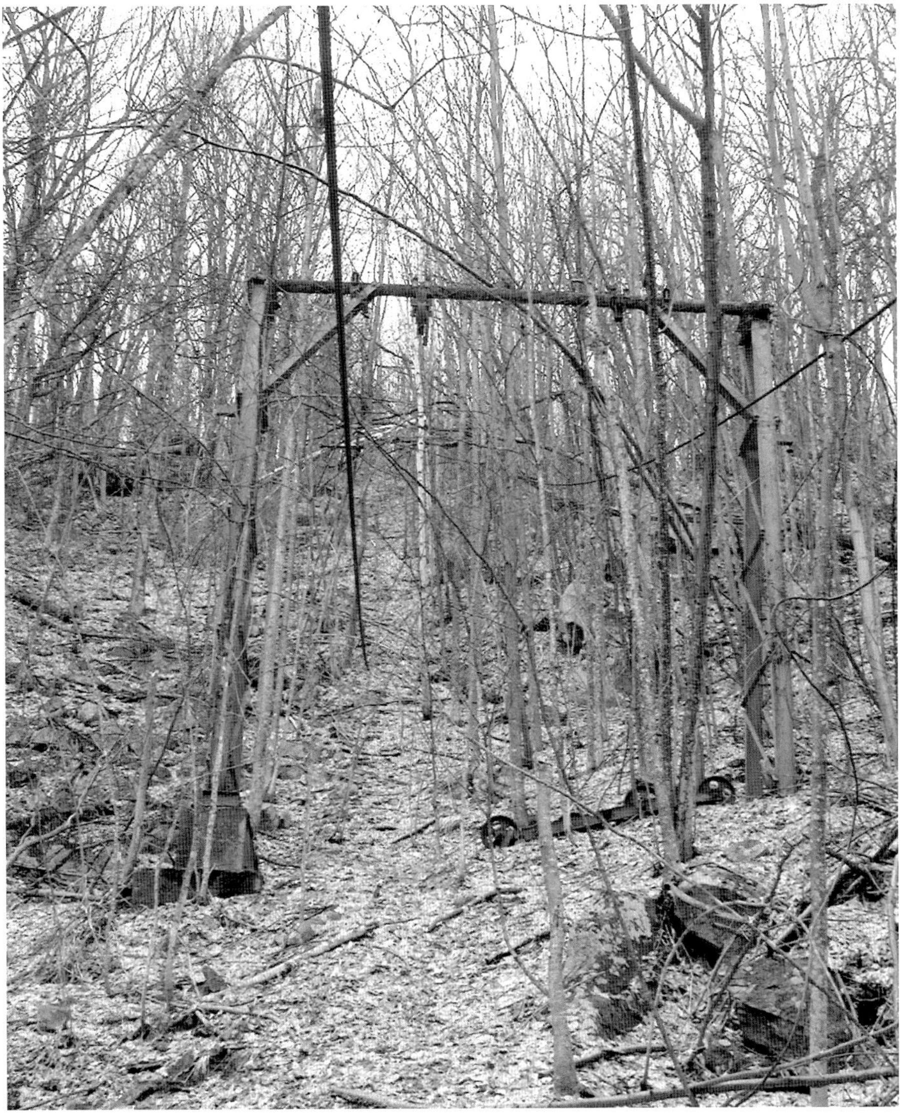

The same T-bar tower as the previous photo from the 1960s was still standing as of 2006. However, the cables had detached from the tower, and all the T-bars had been removed. The lift line had substantially grown in. This lift was removed in 2008 and is now the line for the Hudson Triple Chair.

Although the Ski Bowl was no longer serving skiers, positive developments would soon occur. Gore Mountain opened a tubing park at the Ski Bowl in 2003, near the site of Carl Schaefer's first rope tow. In 2005, a new development plan called the Ski Bowl Village at Gore Mountain was announced, with an agreement with the town of Johnsburg to enable public skiing at the Ski Bowl. A kickoff party was held in June 2006 for this development. In 2007, a triple chairlift replaced the old beginner T-bar, and lift-served skiing returned to the Ski Bowl. Lights were installed for night skiing, and a terrain park was built.

Over the next few years, trails were built to connect the Ski Bowl with Gore Mountain, and a new Ski Bowl Lodge was built, incorporating the old fireplace. In 2010, the old summit T-bar, which had been abandoned for thirty years, was removed, and the new Hudson Triple Chair was built as its replacement. Old trails were cleared out and a few new ones constructed, and the complex reopened on January 29, 2011. Skiers that season had the chance to enjoy terrain that had not been accessible in thirty-five years.

Additional improvements—including more lifts, trails, a nine-hole golf course, a hotel and town houses—have been proposed. Development has progressed, and more information can be found at www.skibowlvillage.com.

Visiting the Area

The North Creek Ski Bowl is located in Ski Bowl Park off Route 28 in North Creek or via ski trails from Gore Mountain.

Schaefer Skiland

North Creek, New York

1937–41 (public), 1941–98 (private), 2011–present (private)

Schaefer Skiland, often referred to as just "Skiland," was the second location of Carl Schaefer's rope tow. Skiland was opened to the public for a few years, from 1936 to 1940, and featured the North Creek Ski School. After it closed to the public in 1940, it remained in operation for family and friends into the 1980s. The tow was then refurbished and opened again for family and friends only for the 2011–12 ski season.

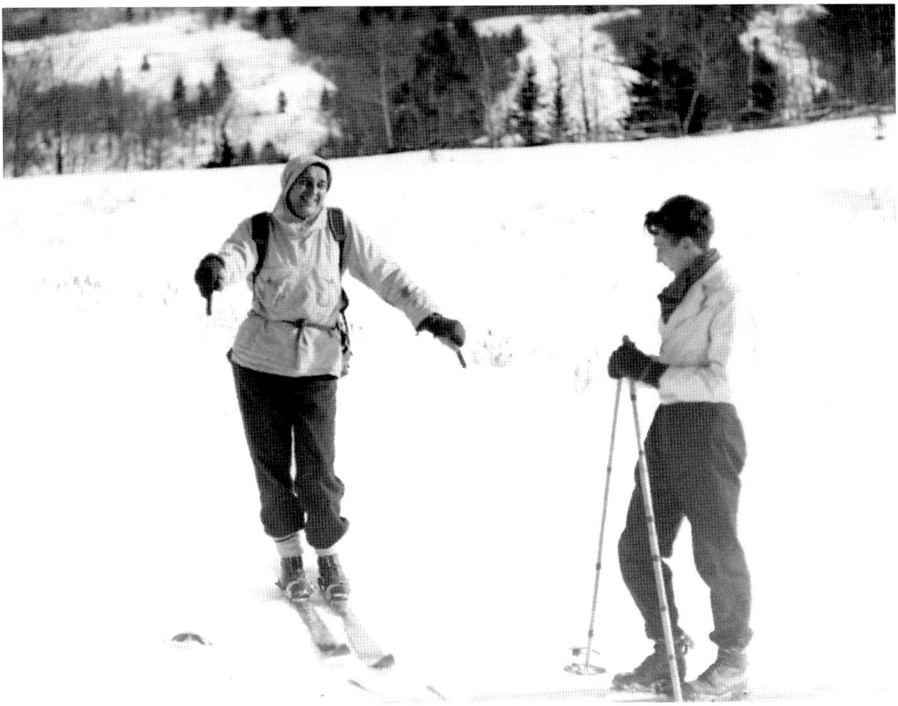

Bill Gluesing (left) and Carl Schaefer (right) are enjoying a sunny day of skiing at Schaefer's Skiland in the late 1930s. Schaefer had moved New York State's first ski tow from the Over the Ridge slopes a few years prior. Gluesing was famous in his own right for coining the phrase "ride up and ski down," which was used prior to the ski lifts, when trucks would haul skiers high up on Gore Mountain's slopes to enjoy a several-mile descent back to North Creek. *Courtesy of Greg Schaefer.*

Carl and Peg Schaefer purchased a property called the Cross Farm just a short distance away from his original rope tow during the summer of 1936. The Cross Slopes had been used for skiing for a few years without a lift. He moved his rope tow to the new property in the fall of 1936 in order to expand his ski school. The motto of the ski school was "If you can walk, we can teach you to ski." Indeed, the ski area was an ideal location to learn, being an expansive bowl with plenty of snow, little wind and away from the crowds.

A youth hostel, the only one of its kind at a ski area, boasted of accommodations for just fifty cents a night. Other facilities included a twenty-meter ski jump, tobogganing, snowshoe rentals and a slalom course.

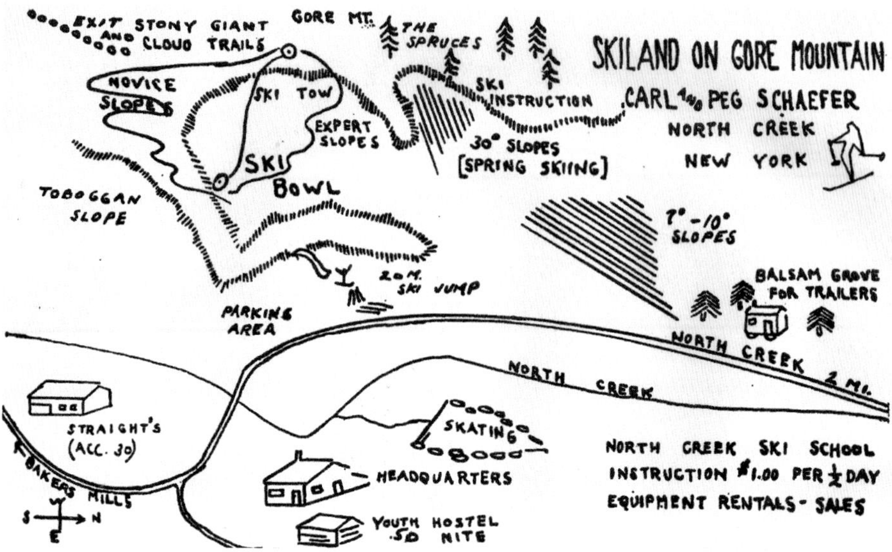

Carl and Peg Schaefer operated Schaefer Skiland for several years after moving their tow from the Village Slopes in 1936. A rope tow served a bowl and expert slopes, while a novice slope and winding trail allowed less experienced skiers the chance to ski from the top. Tobogganing and a twenty-meter jump were also available. A ski dorm provided accommodations at the bargain price of just fifty cents a night. In addition to offering general skiing, Schaefer operated the North Creek Ski School, where a half day of lessons was only one dollar. Also shown here is Straight's, a nearby lodge that would add a rope tow a few years later. *Courtesy of Greg Schaefer.*

Skiland proved very popular for the 1936–37 season and the following one as well. The hostel made the area very attractive for young people, who had a wonderful time at the area. One such skier was Frederica "Freddie" (Woodall) Anderson, who took lessons under Carl Schaefer. As of 2012, she is in her nineties and is a ski instructor at Maple Ski Ridge in Schenectady, having literally taught generations to ski. Thus, Schaefer's legacy of instruction continues to this day.

Tragedy struck Skiland on February 3, 1938, when a fire destroyed the youth hostel and lodge. An electric iron had been left on in the waxing room, which started the blaze and quickly destroyed the lodge and Schaefer's private residence. Schaefer tried to save a few belongings by running into the burning building, and on the last trip, he had to jump from a second-story window to save his life.

Despite losing the hostel, Skiland continued to operate for a few more years as a day area with no lodging available. Then, operations for the public

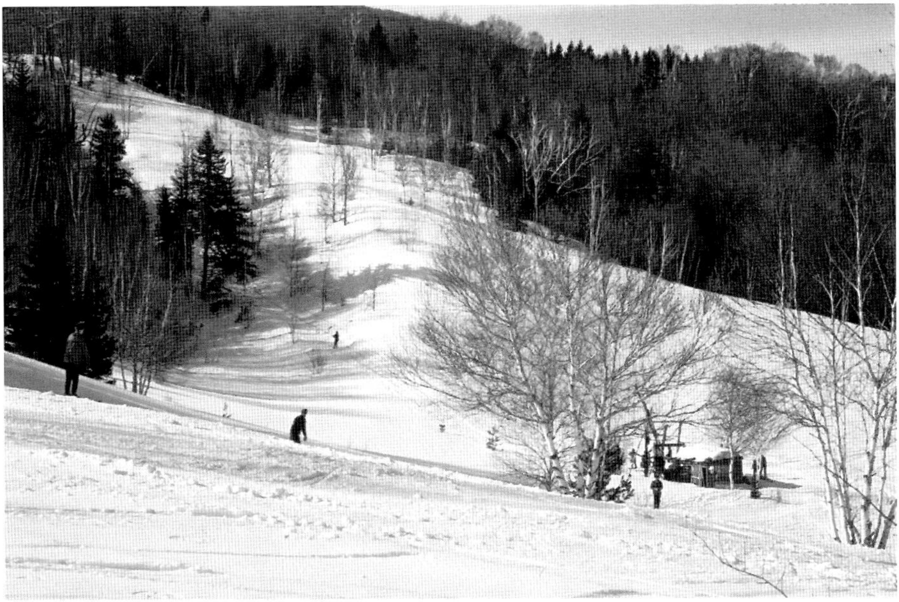

A view of the wide-open slopes at Schaefer's Skiland shows a view of the slopes just prior to the construction of Gore Mountain in the early 1960s. The Gore Mountain access road now slices through the top portion of the slopes shown here. The Skiland was used only by friends and family from 1941 onward. For the 2011–12 season, another rope tow on site was reactivated by the Schaefer family to be used again for family and friends. *Courtesy of Larry Wilke.*

at Skiland wound down for the 1940–41 season. Carl Schaefer needed to be closer to home as a contractor with his brother Paul. Shortly afterward, World War II broke out, and Schaefer became employed with General Electric in Schenectady. For some part-time income, he instructed at Snowhaven in Altamont (another lost ski area) for the remainder of the 1941 season. Skiland was then closed to the public for good.

While no longer open to the public, Skiland did not become abandoned like so many other rope tow ski areas of its time. The family maintained the property as a retreat and kept the tow operational for family and friends from the 1940s into the early 1960s. All of Carl and Peg's children—Pete, Bud (Carl Jr.), Penny, Chris, Greg and Bill—as well as other Schaefer family members grew up skiing at Skiland. Greg Schaefer remembers the area as a young child:

> *At the top of the tow, there were a couple of different ways to come down...a longer way that was nice and gentle through the trees, or there was the steep*

> *shot that went down to the bowl, which was a lot of fun. The cut into the ski area was not always plowed; oftentimes we put food, gas, battery on the toboggan and hauled it to the camp. One group of us would split off and start the fire at the camp while the other would bring the gas and battery to the tow and get it running.*

Major changes affected Skiland in the early 1960s. Plans for a brand-new ski resort on Gore Mountain were drawn up in 1962, including the access road to the mountain. While an engineer's map showed the future access road well above Skiland, Schaefer insisted that the map was incorrect and that the road was going to cut his property in half. An article in the *Albany Times-Union* on January 6, 1963, quoted John K. Bright, who was part of the engineering firm building the road, as saying, "The road, as we have designed it, will pass well above Mr. Schaefer's property." The Warren County Board of Supervisors also confirmed that the road would not touch Schaefer's land. It was soon revealed that the new road would indeed cut into his property, despite these earlier assurances. A lawsuit followed but was not successful, and a portion of Schaefer's property was taken by eminent domain. In 1963, the access road to Gore Mountain was built directly through the upper portion of the rope tow. Lower slopes and the camp at Skiland were both spared. The engine for the rope tow, from the original rope tow in New York State, was left on the hillside just above the access road.

Although this was obviously a major setback for Schaefer, he did not give up. He built another rope tow on the property, this one shorter. Family and friends continued to use the tow until 1998. During that final season, Carl Schaefer skied his final day at Skiland under a bluebird sky. He passed away in 1999, and the tow fell into disuse. The property, however, was passed along to his children, and it is still used as a family retreat.

For the 2011–12 season, the Schaefer family was able to refurbish the tow with a new engine, and thus, Skiland has come back to life, a fitting tribute to Carl Schaefer's vision. The area is open to family and friends only.

Visiting the Area

While the base of Skiland is private, the engine for the rope tow, New York's first, is on public lands just off the Gore Mountain access road. From the start of the access road, drive 0.55 miles and park on the right. The engine is located on the steep slope to the right. The climb is quite a scramble, and the slope is very steep, so please use caution. The engine is located about

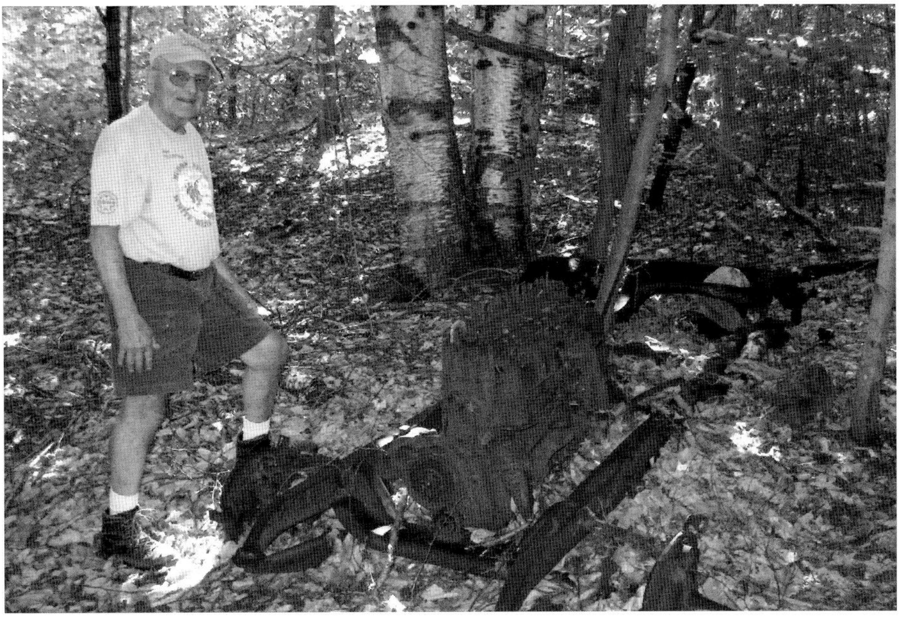

Ski historian Larry Wilke (who had Carl Schaefer as his Scoutmaster as a youth) stands next to the engine that once powered New York State's first rope tow, moved to the Skiland from the Village Slopes. Located just above the Gore Mountain Access Road, it is located up a short but steep scramble. No rope tow towers or pulleys remain from the tow.

150 feet above the road. While visiting, ponder the ski history that this tow brought about—a truly amazing relic from a bygone era!

SCHROON LAKE SKI CENTER

Schroon Lake, New York

1978–88, 2005–resent

After Beech Hill closed in 1951, the Schroon Lake area was left without a community ski center. In 1978, Moe Friedman, who was on the town board, was urging the board to develop recreational activities in town. News came that a Pomalift from Fawn Ridge (a lost ski area in Lake Placid) was available for sale, and Friedman was able to convince the board to purchase it for

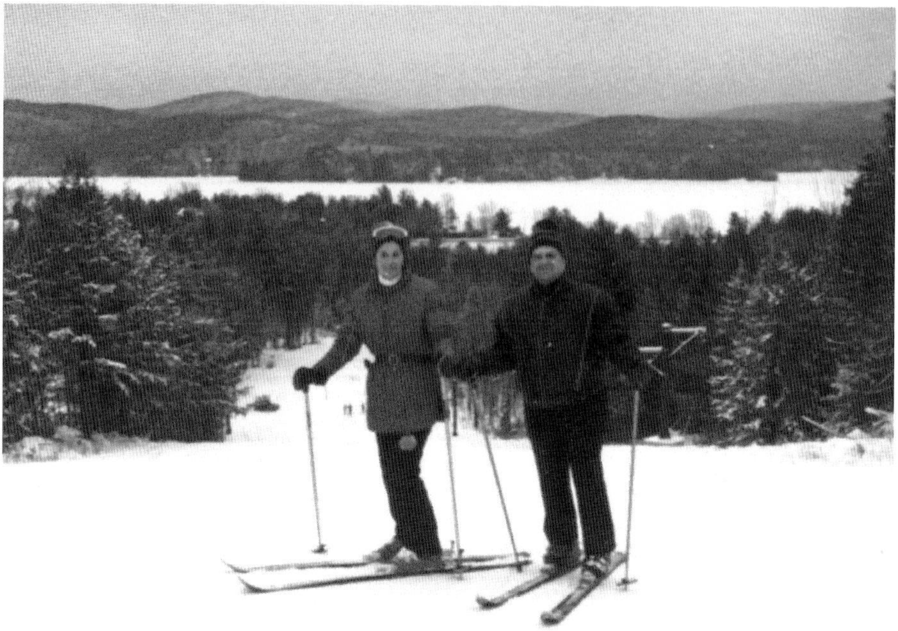

Moe Friedman and his wife, Janet, pose for a photo at the Schroon Lake Ski Center in 1983. The Pomalift, which formerly operated at Fawn Ridge near Lake Placid, can be seen on the edge of the slope. After temporarily closing, the Pomalift was moved to Gore Mountain, where it operates today as the Bear Cub Poma. *Courtesy of the Friedman family.*

$14,000. A matching grant from the New York State Division of Youth contributed toward the cost of the lift and installation.

The next step was to obtain land for a ski slope. Friedman and Dick Drake owned land adjacent to the fourth hole on the town's golf course, and the eight acres was donated to the town. Mike Marnell, the highway superintendent at the time, had his crew clear the slope, smooth and grade it and install the Pomalift. Charles "Buster" Jenks and his son Jeff donated the concrete work, while Robert Kugler provided the necessary engineering on the Pomalift.

The area opened for the 1978–79 ski season, with the town hiring an operator for the tow. The local Lions Club volunteered for other duties at the ski area. The area was very popular with locals and second-home owners, and with free skiing, the area was available to everybody. The ski center also featured a fantastic view of Schroon Lake and Pharaoh Mountain in the distance.

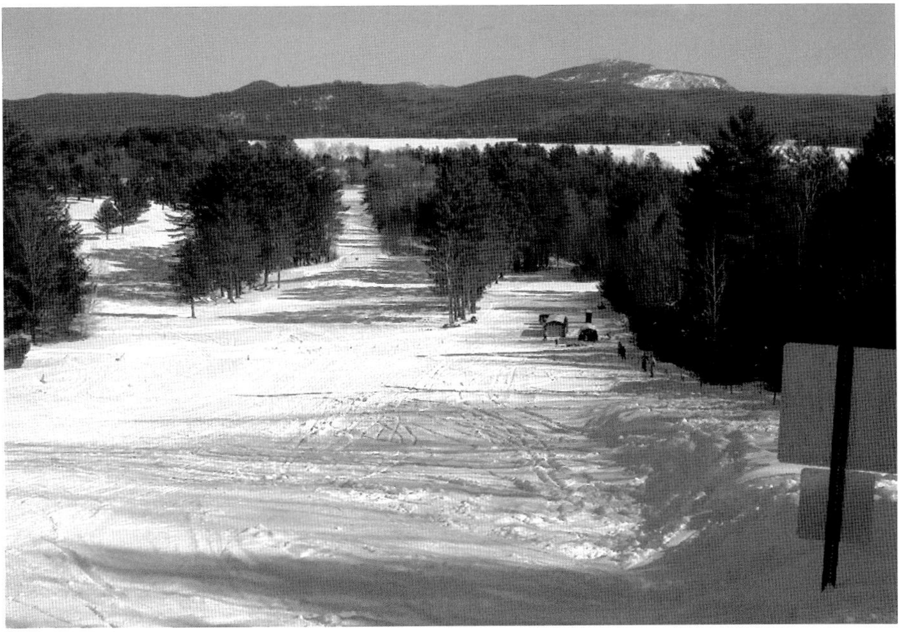

Reopened in 2005, the Schroon Lake Ski Center allows local skiers of all ages to enjoy complimentary skiing on an open slope, served by a handle tow. Vistas of Schroon Lake and Pharaoh Mountain greet skiers and snowboarders at the summit. Affordable opportunities for skiing can be difficult to find, but the Schroon Lake Ski Center is one of the exceptions, and residents can enjoy healthful exercise at the center at no cost.

Skiers enjoyed the center for ten years, until 1988, when insurance costs became too great. In 1996, the lift was removed and given to Gore Mountain for a trade in order to provide complimentary skiing and lessons for the youth of Schroon Lake for five years. The Pomalift still operates today as the Bear Cub lift at Gore.

The slope remained empty until 2004, when a discussion of reopening the ski area began. A grant and funding became available from State Senator Betty Little and Assemblywoman Theresa Sayward to purchase a ski lift and reopen the area. A handle tow was bought and installed by the town highway department. It opened in February 2005, with skiing available on one open slope with a 150-foot drop. A warming hut was also built, with light refreshments available.

Schroon Lake Ski Center continues to be free to the public and is a fun slope to check out. Families particularly enjoy the area, as they can ski for a few hours without the investment of having to purchase a ticket. The area is open mainly on weekends and holidays. Non-skiers can enjoy a tubing area adjacent to the tow (not lift served).

Visiting the Area

Schroon Lake Ski Center is located at the Schroon Lake Golf Course. Follow the "Ski Tow" signs from Route 9 in town. For more information on Schroon Lake and the surrounding area, visit www.schroon.net and www.schroonlakeregion.com.

Chapter 6
Open Ski Areas

The Southern Adirondack region certainly has lost a substantial number of ski areas. However, the region is still filled with plenty of classic ski areas of all sizes. Most of these ski areas offer affordable rates, old-fashioned trails and a family atmosphere. Their continued operation depends on skiers and snowboarders enjoying their slopes and trails.

The following is a general guide to these ski areas; for more information, please visit their websites or call their numbers. For information on the Schroon Lake Ski Center, please see the chapter on restored ski areas.

OPEN SKI AREAS MAP

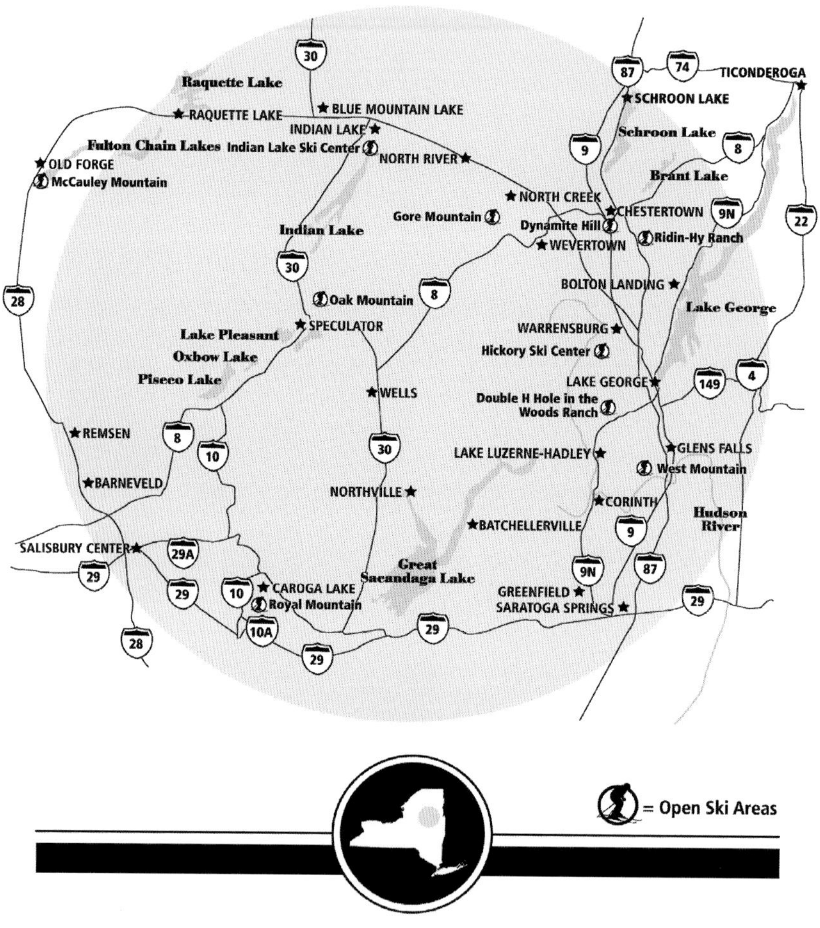

A wide variety of open ski areas is found across the Southern Adirondacks. From classic ski areas such as Hickory Ski Center, to large resorts such as Gore Mountain, to free skiing at Indian Lake, skiers and snowboarders have many choices to enjoy the sport. These open ski areas all carry on the legacy of the lost ski areas throughout the region. *Map designed by Scott Cahill.*

Double H Ranch

Lake Luzerne, New York
www.doublehranch.org
(518) 696-5676
Lifts: 1 double chair
Trails: 2
Vertical Drop: 150 feet

Double H Ranch, founded by Charles R. Wood and Paul Newman, has a wonderful Adaptive Winter Sports Program for children and their families dealing with life-threatening illnesses. Originally, it operated as part of the Hidden Valley Dude Ranch, and when that went up for sale, it was purchased by the Charles R. Wood Foundation. The slope and chairlift are one of the best reaching slopes in the Northeast. It is a private ski area and is not open to the general public, but those who wish to volunteer for the Adaptive Winter Sports Program should contact the ranch directly. Over 150 ski instructors volunteer each year, along with National Ski Patrol volunteers. As the program is free of charge for participants, donations are always welcome.

Dynamite Hill

Chester, New York
www.townofchesterny.org
Lifts: 1 rope tow
Trails: 1
Vertical Drop: 65 feet

Dynamite Hill is the Southern Adirondacks' sole surviving rope tow ski area, located just west of Exit 25 off Interstate 87. Operated by the Town of Chester and the Rotary Club, the ski area features free skiing on weekends and some nights, accessed via a rope tow. For the 2011–12 season, snow making was installed, a rare addition to a rope tow–only ski area. Sledding, skating, snowshoeing and cross-country ski trails are also available.

GORE MOUNTAIN

North Creek, New York
www.goremountain.com
(518) 251-2411
Lifts: 14, including a high-speed gondola and two high-speed detachable chairlifts
Trails: 94, including 19 glades
Vertical Drop: 2,537 feet

Gore Mountain is the largest ski area in the Southern Adirondacks, the second largest in New York State and one of the largest in the East. It features challenging, steep trails, miles of intermediate cruising and easy beginner terrain. Trails have now been connected to the former Ski Bowl, merging the two ski areas. Two base lodges are available, one at the main base and the other at the Ski Bowl.

If you are visiting Gore Mountain, a ride on the Gore Mountain Snow Train (www.goremountainsnowtrain.com) is a must for history buffs. Re-creating the snow trains of the past, the Saratoga and North Creek Railway (www.sncrr.com) restarted snow train service to North Creek for the 2011–12 ski season. Leaving from Saratoga Springs, the train takes about two hours to North Creek, riding along the scenic Hudson River. From North Creek, skiers and snowboarders are transported via shuttle buses to the mountain, where they can enjoy a full day of skiing. At the end of the day, they are shuttled back to the North Creek Depot for the ride back to Saratoga. Be sure to enjoy the North Creek Depot Museum (www.northcreekdepotmuseum.com) and its excellent exhibit on local skiing.

HICKORY SKI CENTER

Warrensburg, New York
www.hickoryskicenter.com
(518) 623-5754
Lifts: 4, including two high-speed detachable Pomalifts
Trails: 18
Vertical Drop: 1,200 feet

Hickory Ski Center is a rare gem among ski areas. As of the writing of this book, it does not have snow making and offers an all-natural ski experience. Easier and intermediate trails are groomed, while expert trails are left to bump up. Only surface lifts, including two high-speed detachable Pomalifts, access the terrain. Hickory's trails are twisty, full of dips and drops and hearken back to the early days of skiing. A comfortable base lodge with a large fireplace is available to guests.

Indian Lake Ski Center

Indian Lake, New York
townofindianlake.org
Lifts: 1 T-bar
Trails: 2
Vertical Drop: 200 feet

Located just south of the town of Indian Lake on Route 30, the Ski Center is usually open on weekends and holidays. Like Dynamite Hill and Schroon Lake, the skiing is free to all and is supported by the town. Two beginner-intermediate slopes are accessed by a Hall T-bar. While there is no snow making, natural snowfall is usually plentiful due to the higher elevation of the ski area.

McCauley Mountain

Old Forge, New York
www.mccauleyny.com
(315) 369-3225
Lifts: 1 double chair, 2 T-bars, 2 rope tows
Trails: 21
Vertical Drop: 633 feet

McCauley Mountain in Old Forge is a terrific family mountain with a wide variety of trails and slopes. Experts will enjoy the difficult Olympic Trail, while the beginner Challenger gradually descends from the summit. The surrounding hills and the Fulton Chain of Lakes are clearly visible from the summit. Average snowfall is a whopping 281 inches due to persistent lake effect snows, leading to many powder days.

Oak Mountain

Speculator, New York
oakmountainski.com
(518) 548-3606
Lifts: 1 quad chair, 2 T-bars
Trails: 14
Vertical Drop: 650 feet

Oak Mountain is a fully modern, medium-sized ski area with recently upgraded facilities. It offers a quad chairlift, snow making, excellent grooming and a large base lodge. Trails remain very similar to when they were constructed, keeping the skiing interesting. Classic ski trail buffs should not miss the S-turns on Kunjamuck or the steep turns of TAG. Rates are affordable, and the mountain features beautiful views of the surrounding landscape.

Ridin-Hy Ranch

Warrensburg, New York
www.ridinhy.com
(518) 494-2742
Lifts: 1 T-bar
Trails: 1
Vertical Drop: 230 feet

The Ridin-Hy Ranch is an all-inclusive family resort with many activities in the winter and summer. It operates a ski area only for guests who are staying at the property on a beginner-intermediate slope served by a T-bar. Other winter sports, including snowshoeing, ice skating, tubing, ice fishing and snowmobiling, are also available.

Royal Mountain

Caroga Lake, New York
www.royalmountain.com
(518) 835-6445
Lifts: 3 double chairs
Trails: 15, including glades
Vertical Drop: 500 feet

Royal Mountain in Caroga Lake offers a wide variety of trails and slopes, from the easy Knight to the plunging T-bar Line trails. Three double chairlifts—two of them new in the past ten years—keep lines to a minimum. A classic base lodge remains a cozy place for skiers to grab a bite to eat or warm up between runs. The area prides itself on meticulous grooming and snow making and is a terrific all-around family ski area.

West Mountain

Queensbury, New York
www.skiwestmountain.com
(518) 793-6606
Lifts: 2 double chairs, 1 triple chair, 1 Magic Carpet, 1 rope tow, 3 tubing tows
Trails: 40
Vertical Drop: 1,010 feet

West Mountain is conveniently located a few miles west of Exit 18 on Interstate 87 and is clearly visible from the highway. The ski area is open seven days a week, with night skiing six days. A combination of wide-open cruising terrain along narrower woods trails provides a full day's worth of interesting skiing. The Westside Grille, on the second floor of the base lodge, offers diners a full view of the lower slopes.

AFTERWORD

Thirty-nine ski areas have been lost across the Southern Adirondack region over the past seventy-five years. All of these areas played an important role in the development of the sport. Many skiers learned to ski, spent family vacations and even met their future spouses while enjoying these areas. Operators had to dedicate almost all their time to keeping them in top condition so that they would be safe and enjoyable for all. These places deserve to be remembered and not forgotten.

Now is the time to preserve their legacy. Lost areas are rapidly fading away, and in a few short decades, very little will be left of them. From using digital cameras to take photos of lost ski area remnants, to scanning in slides and old photographs, to the digitization of newspaper archives, it has never been easier to document and discover lost ski areas.

Many historical societies and museums have worked hard to archive their local skiing history. These include the Adirondack Museum, North Creek Depot Museum, Johnsburg Historical Society, Salisbury Historical Society, New England Ski Museum, Ticonderoga Historical Society (Hancock House), Town of Lake Pleasant and Speculator, Town of Webb (Goodsell Museum) and Warrensburgh Historical Society and Museum. Supporting these organizations ensures that ski history can be preserved for generations to come.

If you enjoyed any of these areas and have memories or photos, it is important to save them. Some skiers think that nobody would be interested in their old photos or ski area materials. Nothing could be further from the truth. If you are considering disposing of old ski memorabilia, be sure to contact your local historical society, museum or town archives, which may accept them as a donation.

Also, the New England/NorthEast Lost Ski Areas Project (www.nelsap.org) is documenting lost ski areas across New York State and beyond. If you wish to contribute historical ski imagery and memories from any area in this book, please visit the website. You will be amazed at how many passionate skiers would enjoy viewing your archives, even if they never skied that particular area.

Perhaps the best way to honor these lost ski areas is to patronize the locations still in operation. So many wonderful opportunities exist across the Southern Adirondacks for downhill skiing. These classic ski areas offer trails for all abilities, lesson programs and affordable prices. Challenge yourself to visit every publicly available ski area throughout the region—you will be glad you did!

BIBLIOGRAPHY

Adirondack Echo (Old Forge, NY), November 11, 1992.

Buxton, John. *Eastern Ski Slopes*. Greenwich, CT: John S. Herold, Inc., 1964.

County Times (Chittenago, NY), January 3, 1974.

Currier (Clinton, NY), March 24, 1973.

Daily Democrat and Record (Amsterdam, NY), January 4, 1958.

Daily Eagle (Brooklyn, NY), January 1941–December 1950.

Daily Press (Utica, NY), January 1936–December 1968.

Davis, Bronny. *Tales of Indian Hill: The Biggest Little Ski Area*. N.p.: Xilbris, 2007.

Dibelius, Norman. *Winter Sports*. Schenectady, NY: Schenectady Wintersports Club, 1995.

Elkins, Frank. *The Complete Ski Guide*. New York: Doubleday, Doran & Company, Inc., 1940.

Federal Writers' Project. *Skiing in the East: The Best Ski Trails and How to Get There*. New York: M. Barrows & Company, 1939.

Free Press (Auburn, NY), December 18, 1958.

Frontier Herald (Blasdell, NY), February 3, 1955.

Herald (Boonville, NY), February 1936–November 1985.

Landman, Joan, and David Landman. *Where to Ski*. Boston: Houghton Mifflin Company, 1949.

Leader Herald (Gloversville-Johnstown, NY), January 1962–December 1964.

Morning Herald (Gloversville, NY), February 1947.

Moro, Mary. *History of Skiing in North Creek and on Gore Mountain*. N.p., n.d.

Niagara Falls Gazette (Niagara Falls, NY), December 17, 1938.

Observer (Utica, NY), January 1936–December 1968.

Pain, William. *The American Ski Directory*. New York: Permabooks, 1961.

Post (New York, NY), February 18, 1943.
Post-Star (Glens Falls, NY), December 1935–March 1944.
Carl F. Schaefer, letter to *North Creek News Enterprise*, August 4, 1997.
Schenectady Gazette (Schenectady, NY), February 1935–December 1995.
Ski New York Brochures, 1939–1970.
Ski New York Guidebooks, 1949–1953.
Ski Train News, February 11, 1936.
Ticonderoga Sentinel (Ticonderoga, NY), February 1936–December 1946.
Times-Union (Albany, NY), January 31, 1988.
Warrensburg–Lake George News (Warrensburg, NY), January 1936–December 1984.

About the Author

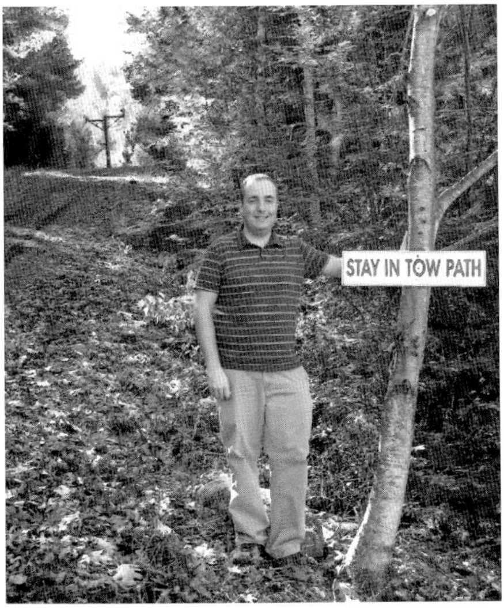

Jeremy Davis is a passionate skier and has enjoyed exploring skiing history from the moment he learned how to ski. A 2000 graduate of Lyndon State College in Vermont, he is a senior meteorologist at Weather Routing Inc. in Glens Falls, New York, where he provides professional weather forecasts to marine clients worldwide. Jeremy has served on the New England Ski Museum's Board of Directors since 2000. His website, the New England/NorthEast Lost Ski Areas Project (www.nelsap.org), has been in operation since 1998, and in 2009, it won the prestigious Cyber Award for best ski history website from the International Ski History Association. He is the author of two books, *Lost Ski Areas of the White Mountains* (2008) and *Lost Ski Areas of Southern Vermont* (2010). He is a member of Ski Venture in Glenville, New York, one of the oldest ski clubs that still operates a rope tow–only ski area. He resides just outside the Adirondacks near Saratoga Springs, New York.